# No Longer Church As Usual

*Restoring first century values and structure to the 21<sup>st</sup> Century Church*

Published by
**KINGDOM WORD PUBLICATIONS**
ALBION, MICHIGAN 49224

Printed in the U.S.A.

KINGDOM WORD PUBLICATIONS is the publishing division of THE CENTER FOR NEW TESTAMENT CHURCH DEVELOPMENT. The mission of KINGDOM WORD PUBLICATIONS is to produce and distribute quality materials that will strengthen believers, and assist in planting and developing churches structured after New Testament patterns.

We pray that these materials will aid in equipping leaders and help to lay firm biblical foundations that exalt the Lord Jesus Christ as He builds His church and extends His Kingdom in the earth.

For more information, visit our website www.ntcdonline.org

NO LONGER CHURCH AS USUAL

*Restoring first century values and structure to the 21st Century Church*

ISBN 978-0-9712916-9-0
Library of Congress Control Number: 2010903108

Unless otherwise noted, all Scripture references are taken from the King James Version of the Bible

All references to satan and the devil are not capitalized in this book, even when it is literarily proper to do so.

I have known Tim Kurtz for several years now. He and I have spent countless phone hours discussing his heart's passion, the true New Testament Church. Because of these phone calls I have been given the privilege of inclusion on the formation of "No Longer Church as Usual."

All of my ministry I have heard numerous times, "The New Testament is rather quiet when it comes to how we 'do church!'" Without a doubt, Tim Kurtz completely debunks that myth with a step by step, systematic exposure of New Testament foundational truth. With block upon block, Kurtz builds to the ultimate climax of Chapter 13, "The Kingdom Mandate!" My suggestion to anyone interested in advancing the Kingdom of God, get this book, meditate on it, pray about it, implement it, for you won't be sorry you did!

**Dr. Larry and Corinne Silverman**
**Revivalists To Today's Generation**
**Beverly Hills, Florida**


WOW!!! Even though Paul witnessed the beginning of the decline of the church, he was not disappointed or discouraged. Because he had both insight and foresight, he could be encouraged. He knew that some day and somehow the church would reach God's standard. The majority of the believers may decline, but a small number at least would be chosen, preserved, and established to practice 'the church life' according to the divine standard.

I thank God for His wisdom in imparting such revelation, illumination, into our dear friend Apostle Tim Kurtz. I do firmly believe that this is an essential part of God revealing his heart and mind that will funnel His original intent.

*But if I tarry long, that thou mayest know how thou oughtest to behave thyself (**function**) in the house of God, which is the church of the living God, the pillar and ground of the truth. And without controversy great is the mystery of godliness: God was manifest in the flesh, justified in the Spirit, seen of angels, preached unto the Gentiles, believed on in the world, received up into glory* (1Timothy 3:15-16)

Shepherd Donald R. and Lavella Todd
Impact Ministries
Lansing, Michigan

"NO LONGER CHURCH AS USUAL" is a powerful tool for anyone who truly wants to explore and discover biblical foundations for the governing of authentic gatherings of believers that will be a part of the advancing Kingdom of God here in earth as in heaven! Tim Kurtz's balance and passion for this topic is refreshing; yet totally challenging to practices that have hindered the church for far too long! The government of our Father God and King Jesus are arising like never before that He (King Jesus) might continue to build HIS CHURCH!

True biblical order has always been there for us in the scriptures. Thank God for using Brother Tim to serve us all into the possibilities that come with seeing things even clearer.

If you have known in your heart that there must be more than what you've known of "Church" then "NO LONGER CHURCH AS USUAL" will be a wonderful workable tool for living out the principles found in scripture about "The Church". If you really want more and are willing to humbly change for the glory of God the Father and his True

Church; the body of the King, Jesus the Christ; this is a book that will be a tremendous blessing in your life.

Donald L. Coleman
Church of the Nations,
Co-Founder East End Fellowship
and OASIS East
Richmond, Virginia


I believe this book is a *revelation word* from God. It is designed to open up an awareness to people who feel they are hearing God say, "...there is a move to advance the kingdom, and not just the church". For too long the church has been a solid mass set in one place – not reaching the masses. In reality it is a liquid that can flow into every crack and crevice of life. In "the church" people have ministries given to them by God for the advancement of the kingdom – not just for sitting on a seat while one person does all the talking. When 'this gospel of the kingdom' has been preached in all the world, then the end shall come!

Richard Fowlkes
Crewe, Virginia

# TABLE OF CONTENTS

# ACKNOWLEDGEMENTS

The more I write, the more I am convinced that it is impossible to write a book alone. This book is no exception. God trusted me with this revelation, and then surrounded me with great people who provided insight and guidance in the formulation of this work. This is my thank you to these individuals.

In this day and age, revelation without counsel can be dangerous. Thomas Beale, Don Coleman, Richard Fowlkes, Donald Todd and Thomas Wynn, Jr. were instrumental in helping me remain articulate and focused. Their reviews of my manuscripts, subsequent personal conversations and prayers are beyond measure. Tony Fournier became a divine connection at a strategic time in this book's development. I will be eternally grateful for the hours he dedicated to reviewing this work with me – page by page. The Lord knew that our connection would be vital, necessary and most of all, encouraging.

Two years ago the Lord instructed me to 'pour into my elders'. For nearly two years we met, prayed and discussed the principles of this work. Alfred Taylor, Joseph Kurtz and Carl Hunt allowed me to teach them these ideas and insights. As foreign as the concepts of this book are to the traditional church, each of these men allowed the Holy Spirit to speak to their hearts, "Fear not, to [receive this revelation]: for [this] is of the Holy Ghost (Matthew 1:20). Their questions and candor helped me to think and rethink the implications this book may have on the local church. I am honored to serve with them.

I greatly appreciate the deacons and ministry team of New Life Ministries International. They have remained patient and strong during this season of my personal development, even though my direct time with them has been limited. Without them, we can never be the prototype work the Lord has called us to be.

For some time I have told New Life Ministries International that we are a *New Testament – Apostolically Governed – Pioneering Church*. On our stage we have a banner that reads "No Longer Church As Usual". God has blessed me with an eclectic group of saints who are embracing this God given mandate. They make having a unique revelation easy.

The Lord sent Kat Wheeler at the right time. She quickly and expertly reviewed the manuscript to help address the little things we most often miss. What a wonderful gift she is to the Body of Christ.

Finally, everyone reading this book must understand how I love and appreciate my wife, Carolyn. For months, she has graciously allowed me to disappear days at a time in my office to work on this project. She has patiently heard the details of this book more than anyone. She prays for me all the time. She is a constant source of encouragement to me. Therefore in the words taken from the movie *As Good As it Gets*, "[She] makes me want to be a better man".

In the end, I [praise God] for what he has given, which words have no power to say (2Corinthians 9:15 Bible in Basic English).

TIM

# FOREWORD

About three years ago I received a call from a gentleman in Albion Michigan named Timothy Kurtz. He had gotten my name and contact info from a brother in Philadelphia who told him that he needed to get in touch with me to further explore what God had placed in his heart concerning the church and its practices.

I am eternally grateful for receiving that call. On it, I heard a seasoned church leader who for years had done things according to the traditions that were handed down to him, and was now hearing God speaking something to his heart that was totally different from everything he had ever been taught or had ever experienced.

This conversation changed both of our lives. For Tim it was affirmation that what Father was speaking into his heart wasn't isolated or marginalized, but instead was something that He was speaking into the hearts of countless others who have a sincere desire to see Father's Kingdom come and Father's will be done on earth as it is in heaven. As for me, that conversation was the beginning of a wonderful relationship that has enriched my journey with Christ tremendously. Through Tim I witnessed a balanced approach to truly implementing and living out biblical structure in the church of Jesus Christ.

In your hands you are holding more than a collection of thoughts and ideas by a person who assumes to have some sort of spiritual accruement or insight on a particular subject matter. You are holding a window. A window that Father has allowed Tim to peer out of and look right into His heart concerning the structure of His church. Like most things that come straight from Father's heart into our lives (by the power of His Spirit), this window has completely captivated, consumed, challenged and changed Tim's life forever. Now Father has directed Tim to make this window available to you. It is my hope that the view that it affords you will impact your life just as strongly.

Through this window you will see how the Lord originally intended for His body to relate to Him, to one another and to the world. Through this window you will also see how the Lord intended for leadership to relate to and flow within His church. And lastly, the view from this window will give you a unique opportunity to examine God's divine structure for His church that will equip, position and propel every member of His body to reach their fullest potential in Christ Jesus.

This window that you now hold in your hands will consequently afford you an amazing opportunity to objectively view  the church as we've known and practiced it, and at the same time see Father's will for the church He desires to build as found in scripture. From these two perspectives you will see that a lot of what we have done in the church is not in scripture, and conversely, a lot of what is in scripture has not been truly practiced in the church.

These two views – our view and God's view of the church – will most likely leave you with one question: Where do we go from here? This book – this window – gives an excellent answer to that question. And if at the end of your viewing you decide to do what Tim Kurtz and countless others have done after witnessing the glorious sights that are seen through this window (that is – jump out of the window to experience the joy and fulfillment that awaits you  on the other side), rest assured that the Spirit of Christ will guide you safely and lovingly right into the middle of God's eternal will for the body of His Son, the Glorious Church of which you are a vital part ....Enjoy the view!

Thomas L. Wynn, Jr.
MARCH 2010

# INTRODUCTION

*And I say also unto thee, That thou art Peter, and upon this rock I will build my church; and the gates of hell shall not prevail against it. (Matthew 16:18)*

*And when the day of Pentecost was fully come, they were all with one accord in one place. (Acts 2:1)*

*And they, continuing daily with one accord in the temple, and breaking bread from house to house, did eat their meat with gladness and singleness of heart, Praising God, and having favour with all the people. And the Lord added to the church daily such as should be saved. (Acts 2:46-47)*

*... even as Christ also loved the church, and gave himself for it; That he might sanctify and cleanse it with the washing of water by the word, <u>That he might present it to himself a glorious church, not having spot, or wrinkle, or any such thing; but that it should be holy and without blemish.</u> (Ephesians 5:25-27 KJV)*

The Church has a glorious destiny. For now however, the Church that the Lord decreed to Peter, and was birthed at Pentecost, is still being built. For nearly a decade, the Lord has been showing me bits and pieces of His Church as He continues to build it.

He has shown me a church structured remarkably different from any church most of us are familiar with. It is a church wherein the saints are released and activated to do the work of ministry. It is a church where you have the freedom to pursue God's purpose for your life. It is a church embracing the values and modeling the structure of the first century church. It is a Glorious Church that He will present to Himself without spot or wrinkle. It is a church historically demonstrated throughout the pages of the New Testament. I believe it is the church He is looking for today.

Jesus is still building His Church. What took place on The Day of Pentecost was only the beginning. For nearly two thousand years the Lord has continued to build His Church – His way. The bumps and turns along the way were the attempts of the enemy to thwart the reality of this moment. This is the season when all is in place to release millions of saints to 'do the work of ministry' and 'turn the world upside down'. But it will require making changes to the way we approach 'church' today.

The process that leads to any change begins with an idea. That idea can be birthed from human ingenuity or divine revelation. It then becomes the task of the progenitor of the idea to 'write the vision or idea' in such terms that anyone who reads it can find a place for themselves within it. That has been a goal resting in my spirit from the first day I sat down and began writing this book. Somewhere, in the pages that follow, I pray you will see yourself activated in the Lord's church – not simply to usher, sing in the choir or volunteer for committees – but active in changing lives and expanding the Kingdom of God in the earth.

In November of 2006, after years of thinking about and researching the church, I wrote and presented the first outline of what you will read in this book. The *Vision for the 21ˢᵗ Century Church* was a paper presented to the leaders of my church. Looking back, in 2006 I still had difficulty articulating what I was seeing in my spirit. But it was clearly a time when a shift was taking place in my spirit that brought definition to what the Lord was showing me.

My burden is for the traditional or institutional church. I deeply desire to see churches that will completely release believers to impact the world – not through programs and events, but through an army of interdependent believers who thoroughly understand the Kingdom Mandate and are willing to aggressively pursue it within their sphere of influence.

Many books have been written about the 'house church', 'simple church' and 'organic church' movements. I have been blessed to read many of them. Most of them minister to individuals who are not actively involved in the traditional or institutional church. I do not believe God's purpose in this season will overlook the church as we know it. I believe God is speaking to the hearts of men and women in the existing church to change. It is my prayer that No Longer Church As Usual will be a small catalyst in providing a roadmap for that change.

I Call You Blessed,

Tim Kurtz
January 2010

# I Know What You Did Last Sunday

If you went to 'church' last Sunday, you probably experienced some variation of the same event that took place millions of times in other churches throughout this country.

Most churches began their worship service around 11 a.m. following some form of Christian education or Sunday School. Choirs or Praise Teams heralded the beginning of the worship experience. You may have read through responsive readings found in the back of a hymnal or you may have quoted some responsive spiritual chants.

"Oh Lord, open thou our lips," one would say, "And our mouths shall show forth thy praise," the congregation responds. In another church the Pastor or one of his assistants would say, "The Lord is in His Holy Temple, let all the earth keep silence before Him." Ironically, instead of silence, a choir or some variation of an organ (pipe or

Hammond B3) would break the silence to usher you into your weekly worship experience.

The highlight of the worship was either a solemn reception of the Eucharist or a message by the Pastor. Peppered in-between there was an offering, a special performance by the choir, dance troop or soloist. Depending on your religious 'flavor', you either sat quietly throughout these events or you were on your feet, clapping your hands, shouting the praises of God, and oh yes, speaking in tongues. Of course, announcements were made to alert you to activities that would be held throughout the week.

By one o'clock or so you were dismissed to rush home to dinner or to your local favorite restaurant. In your mind you felt you received your spiritual diet for the week. During the upcoming week, you may be committed to a choir rehearsal, a men's or women's group, or some other program or event. You may regularly attend a mid-week 'bible study' or 'worship service'. Your interaction with other believers in your church would most likely be limited to these activities.

In some churches, you may be involved in a 'cell group' or some other form of small groups that may meet in homes. The agenda for your small group may be limited to studying the pastor's message or it may serve as a support group for various issues (divorce, addictions, grief, single parents, etc.). Depending on your church guidelines, you may be required to 'multiply' your group in order to help your church grow. You may be limited to meeting on a specific night each week and be required to report your activities to an assigned Pastor or regional leader. No offerings are allowed, and problems need to be reported to those in charge of the church's cell or small group program.

If you are not the Pastor, an elder, deacon, board member, trustee or paid staff member, you are unlikely to think about how your church functions. Budgets, salaries, overhead expenses and building funds are not things you fret over throughout the week. You pay your tithe and give your offering and usually don't think much about where the money is going.

You don't think about preparing a message to preach, or find yourself on call 24/7 for the needs of 'your flock'. If you hear about a need a specific member has, you may gladly join in prayer with others for their relief and generally expect your pastor to handle the matter.

This is a general overview of the majority of churches across this country. To most believers, this all seems to be normal. You may have recognized some things that you personally do in your church. I doubt if you see anything out of place, and you most likely will do the same thing you have always done next Sunday.

## WE LIVE BY THE WORD OF GOD...

We claim that everything we do is biblically based. But is it? You sit week after week in a pew or chair (depending on whether you worship in a Cathedral or Worship Center), and you watch the spiritual activities that unfold on the platform before you. Your participation is primarily limited to 'watching' rather than 'participating'. You assume that it is the biblical way of 'doing church'.

The variation of your worship regardless of denominational affiliation has been taught to you explicitly or implicitly by tradition and reinforced by your pastor. Your pastor was taught the same thing either by church tradition, seminary or both. You have always understood that some in the church were 'clergy' and others were 'laymen'. The clergy were the spiritual elite who instructed and ruled over the lay people.

You honor your Pastors (and rightly so considering the responsibilities they have). After all, you have been taught that the pastor or priest was the spiritual expert you could depend on for marriages, funerals, spiritual counseling, visiting the sick, overseeing communion, baptizing new converts and of course preaching every week while simultaneously administering the financial details of the church. But is that really biblical?

NO LONGER CHURCH AS USUAL is not an attack on the church as we know it, but rather it is a revelation of the next phase of the church already described in scripture

Speaking of communion – you may possibly be in a church that 'celebrates' the Lord's Supper once a month during a special service, or you may be of a tradition that receives communion or the Eucharist every Sunday. Regardless of your tradition, you probably expect the Lord's Supper to be a solemn quiet event where you eat a tasteless little cracker and drink a thimble full of grape juice (or possibly wine). But once again, is a silent solemn ceremony biblical?

One thing you always expect is the offering time. You have become audibly immune to the plethora of scriptures used to convince you to turn loose your money to the church. You give your tithes and offerings and know it is being used to pay clergy salaries, building funds, youth funds, equipment funds and much more. You may even give to a 'benevolence' fund in case there are those in need among you. These of course may be admirable causes, but is giving in this manner biblical?

Questioning whether these familiar activities are biblical may prepare you for the rest of this book. To be clear, NO LONGER CHURCH AS USUAL is not an attack on the church as we know it, but rather it is a revelation of the next phase of the church already described in scripture.

We usually do what we understand. Prayerfully this book will give you a greater understanding and appreciation for the glorious church Jesus said He would build.


## THE CHURCH IS IN TRANSITION

The Lord is bringing His Church to maturity. It is a high level of maturity that will require a total change in the mind of believers. It is not change just to change. It is change to produce a stronger and more powerful church. It is change to fulfill the purposes of God in the earth.

This transition is a reformation. It is a reformation that will restore New Testament values and structure. It is a reformation that will aggressively reactivate the biblical mandate to be fruitful, multiply, replenish and subdue the earth.

There have been many names attributed to this transition. Some call it the Saints Movement, or the Day of the Saints. Others focus on the structure of the church calling this season the time of the House Church, Organic Church or Simple Church. You will find that it is a combination of all of these. It is the saints finding new life in churches that gather in the homes of believers just as they did in the first century church. It is the empowerment gained by many churches coming together to solidify a collective divine purpose. It is a body of believers who are learning the purposes of God through on-going training and building. It is the church Jesus said He would build; a church which the gates of hell would have no power to defeat. (Matthew 16:18; Ephesians 3:10).

## A PRESENT TRUTH REVELATION

*Wherefore I will not be negligent to put you always in remembrance of these things, though ye know [them], and be established in the present truth (2Peter 1:12).*

Jesus declared that we should not live by bread alone, but by every Word that continues to proceed from God. In other words, what God said in the past was powerful truth we must embrace, yet what He is saying now becomes the revelation that produces our daily bread (Matthew 4:4; 6:11). To be clear, whatever God says now will in no way refute what He has said earlier. No revelation can supersede His written word. So then, what is God saying now?

*And he gave some, apostles; and some, prophets; and some, evangelists; and some, pastors and teachers; <u>For the perfecting of the saints, for the work of the ministry</u>, for the edifying of the body of Christ: (Ephesians 4:11-12)*

The Holy Spirit is bringing emphasis to the 'work of ministry by the saints' in this season. The 'work of ministry' is simply the expansion of the Kingdom of God in the earth through the on-going making of disciples. The 'work of ministry' is done by the believers or the saints who have been trained and equipped by five-fold ministry gifts.

However, the 'work of ministry' cannot be accurately accomplished outside of the biblical structure it was designed to function within.

The New Testament gives us a vivid picture of how the church functioned in the first century. Apostles and Elders governed the church (Acts 20:17, 28; 1Peter 5:1-2). Apostles, Prophets, Evangelists, Pastors and Teachers worked to bring maturity to the church (Acts 13:1; Ephesians 4:11-13). As a result, the massive body of believers expanded throughout the regions (Acts 2:41; 4:4; 6:7).

Instead of meeting in dedicated buildings, the believers gathered in homes (1Corinthians 16:19; Colossians 4:15). There wasn't a pastor officiating the gathering, instead the believers encouraged, exhorted and edified each other (Romans 15:14; Hebrews 10:24-25). The way believers gathered was not a doctrine, but rather the lifestyle of the first century believers.

NO LONGER CHURCH AS USUAL will explore these first century practices and show why they are yet valid today. No, this book does not advocate a reversion to togas and sandals, but rather a return to the principles and practices employed by believers in the first century.

# What Does It Look Like? 2

What does it look like? This is a question asked often by one of our ministers. She teaches that whatever revelation you have, it must be articulated in language that can be visualized by those who hear it. Habakkuk wrote that *'the vision must be written and made plain'* so 'the reader can *'run with it'* (Habakkuk 2:2).

NO LONGER CHURCH AS USUAL explores church structure as seen in the New Testament. This is a book revealing how the expression of first century values, principles and practices can look in the twenty-first century. This is the purpose of this chapter. It is a simple story revealing a twenty-first century church in action. It is a story that demonstrates values, principles and practices of the first century church. It is this story that will set the stage for the remainder of this book.

## It's about six forty–five Thursday evening

Bill and Marci arrive a few moments early at the home of Brett and Carolyn. Marci is toting one of her locally famous punch bowl cakes. A few moments later Janet, a single mother of three, arrives with her children with a fresh tossed salad. By seven–fifteen several others have arrived, some with children, and each with a dish to pass. The last ones to arrive are Jack and Cindy. Jack's friend Doug came with them. He had been invited by Jack to join them that evening.

The dinner was delicious. Doug noted the large loaf of bread in the center of the dining room table next to a large goblet of what appeared to be grape juice. He specifically noted that during the meal no one ate any of the bread or took any of the contents of the cup. He also noted that everyone had a great time of fellowship during the meal.

Shortly after eight P.M., Brett slipped into the living room and started playing a CD of worship music. One by one everyone filed into the living room and began to worship with the music. It doesn't take long for everyone to become totally immersed in the praise and worship. Doug, Jack's guest, appears a little uncomfortable with the situation, and at the same time intrigued by the obvious sincerity of everyone in the room – including the children.

As the praise comes to a beautiful conclusion, Sam offers a prayer of thanksgiving and gives a word of encouragement to the group. There is an additional time of worship as different ones in the group began singing and the others join in. Then sporadically, others in the group share encouraging words and insights from the bible. When it ends, Hanna, one of the wives in the group gathers the children and they go back into another room in the house. Throughout the evening, they can be heard intermittently laughing and singing.

Jack introduces his friend Doug from work. Doug had confided in Jack about problems he was having in his marriage. He had asked Jack to pray for him. When Jack invited him to worship with him, he accepted the invitation expecting to meet him at a local church building (the kind with steeples and pews). The house setting was foreign to him but the atmosphere was surprisingly relaxed. It didn't take Doug long to open up and tell the group his problems.

One by one, members of the group gave Doug words of wisdom and encouragement from various scriptures and personal testimonies. Doug was obviously moved by the love and empathy he received from the group.

By nine thirty, the fellowship began to wind down and the group members began praying for each other. Doug wasn't singled out as the sole object of prayer, instead he shadowed Jack as he prayed for others in the group and others prayed for him.

In the midst of this prayer time, Hanna and the children rejoined the group. Brett then announced that Hanna and her husband Bill had been praying about starting a gathering in their home. In their quest, they completed the orientation offered for those praying about becoming house church leaders. There was a mixture of applause and hugs. The entire group encircled Bill and Hanna and laid hands on them, praying that God will bless them. Bill and Hanna thanked the group for committing to support their efforts.

Brett shared some information regarding the upcoming whole church meeting he had received from the elders. He then took the large loaf of bread that had remained on the dining room table and began breaking pieces and sharing it with the group. He prayed and thanked God for the presence of Christ in their midst. Bill joined in with a prayer thanking God for each person in the group and how much they contributed to each other.

Bill then took a small drink from the goblet that was on the table, and one by one, it was passed around the entire group. Doug was taken aback by this activity, yet when the goblet was handed to him, he felt compelled to partake. He later remarked to Jack that he really felt a part of the group when he did.

As they were leaving, a couple of the guys invited Doug to join them for a round of golf on Saturday. Doug also overheard one of the ladies thank another one for filling in as a chaperone for her children's upcoming field trip at school because of her work schedule. It seemed to Doug that the gathering that evening was the segue to a week of 'family like' activities among those present.

Similar scenarios took place all over town that night and throughout the week. Believers gathered in homes in the region and fellowshipped with each other, ministered to each other, encouraged each other, exhorted each other, broke bread and found ways to meet each others needs.


## FAST FORWARD THREE WEEKS...

On Friday evening, elders and their wives from around the area met for their monthly fellowship dinner. Arthur, one of the elders previously selected to moderate the group gave an outline of the agenda and schedule for the next day. It was obviously going to be a full day.

The elders were joined Saturday morning at breakfast by prophets, evangelists, pastors and teachers who regularly ministered throughout the churches and taught classes for developing leaders.

Nearly every church leader was present and a few itinerant ministers attended. After breakfast, they had a powerful time of prayer. It was clear the Holy Spirit was present.

At ten or so Arthur signaled for the meeting to begin.

The group first tackled some doctrinal issues. After some lively discussion, a consensus was arrived at and the matters were put in writing to be shared with all the church leaders.

The elders and ministers then focused on the public recognition of several new leaders who would be planting churches in their homes. A few of the prophets and teachers each gave testimony of their interaction with these new leaders. It was satisfying to the elders and everybody present to see the churches multiply so effectively. They agreed that all the new leaders would be publicly recognized that weekend.

A schedule of training sessions that would be held during the coming month was reviewed. Several new classes were being added to the schedule geared towards developing a deeper understanding of biblical doctrine. Everyone was pleased with these additions.

Finally, the elders reviewed the financial reports submitted by the deacons. They shared how the Holy Spirit had miraculously leveraged their resources to meet many needs among the people. After some minor adjustments, the elders approved a budget for the deacons to cover the next month. The elders, along with the entire group present, agreed to send financial support to the apostle who had established them in order to assist him in his work in other regions. The group then dispersed until the evening service.

Saturday evening was electrifying. Several dozen churches throughout the region gathered for a time of corporate celebration.

Musicians, youth and adult dance ministries and drama teams ministered at this gathering. Sixteen individuals who had been prayerfully recognized by the elders were brought before the whole church and had hands laid on them to publicly recognize them as the leaders of new church plants. After a musical selection by a youth group, two of the ministers delivered powerful messages and several people were ministered to at the altar.

Sunday morning, a larger crowd gathered for worship. Approximately fifteen hundred people, members of the two hundred or more churches in the area came – all expecting a great move of the Lord. The praise and worship was phenomenal. One of the elders brought an inspiring message and several people who were visiting gave their hearts to the Lord.

> Your method of gathering has a tremendous effect on the results you get. It makes a difference in your life whether you are watching a performance from a pew or personally involved in changing lives

At the close of service the elders gave an opportunity for everyone to give an offering that would be sent to support the work of the founding apostle and his team.

## THE CHURCH IN ACTION...

You have just had an imaginary but very real visit to the church of our Lord Jesus Christ as seen in the New Testament. You have just had a glimpse of the twenty-first century version of the first century church seen in the book of Acts. It is a composite of the fluid, simple and organic churches that met in the homes of believers, and the institutional churches we currently have.

We began with a church gathering that could easily have been held in your home. You saw how the believers' had fellowship, broke bread and effectively ministered to each other. Then you were given a glimpse of the meeting of the leadership as they grappled with the oversight of the whole church. You learned that there were classes you could attend to deepen your doctrinal understanding and gain insight to 21$^{st}$ century church leadership. You experienced the excitement of the multitude of saints who gathered Saturday night and Sunday morning for corporate worship as the whole church.

Finally, even though you did not see the apostle who planted this powerful church, you may have been among those who willingly gave to support his work in other regions.

## CAN THIS TYPE OF CHURCH EXIST TODAY?

Imagine being part of a vibrant, loving, committed gathering of believers who don't simply go to church, but instead who understand they are the church. The Holy Spirit is bringing emphasis to the work of ministry being done by the saints (Ephesians 4:11-12). This is the next sequential event towards the church becoming 'a mature man in the stature of the fullness of Christ' (Ephesians 4:13).

A major part of this restoration is how well you understand the structure of the church. Your method of gathering has a tremendous effect on the results you get. It makes a difference in your life whether you are watching a performance from a pew or personally involved in changing lives. Those who are taught to be laity will not serve as one who is taught to be clergy. You have very little spiritual authority as a spectator. You must have the opportunity to do the work.

NO LONGER CHURCH AS USUAL gives you a panoramic view of what the church should look like. It is not a church of programs and events or liturgy by laity. It is a beautiful Church where Jesus is Lord, where only the Holy Spirit directs the daily activities, and where the forces of darkness are brought to nothing as believers fulfill the Kingdom Mandate.

# What Do We Call It? 3

The gathering in the previous chapter was a result of believers who clearly understood the Church. They did not see the Church as a weekly corporate gathering in a dedicated building. Neither did they see the Church as just a small group bible study that met weekly. They had the deep revelation that they were the Church that Jesus Christ is building.

They understood that individually they were lively stones that collectively form a spiritual house (1Peter 2:5). They understood that they were apostolically and prophetically built together to form a habitation of God through the Spirit (Ephesians 2:22). They embraced the truth that they were many members but one body (1Corinthians 12:20). More importantly they understood that their weekly gathering was a time set aside for their 'spiritual family' to come together. The gathering was in fact a culmination of the interconnected lives they live throughout the week.

It is important that you understand that the church is not a building or a weekly get–together. The church is not choirs, ushers or dynamic preachers. The church is not programs, events or fund raisers for noble causes. The church is life with purpose. It is life lived among the saints who see themselves as family. It is life among believers who understand that they are one body, and that each member is significant to the purposes of God in the earth. This is the Church demonstrated in the New Testament.

For nearly 1,700 years the Lord's Church has been buried in ritual, hierarchy, religious politics, denominationalism and carnal imaginations. But now, the vibrant Church in the New Testament is finding new expression in the twenty-first century. As the Lord pours out His Spirit on all flesh, old men are beginning to dream dreams, young men are seeing visions, sons and daughters are prophesying about the Church (Joel 2:28-29; Acts 2:17-18). They are seeing a church structured like the church in the first century. It is a church that is fruitful, multiplying, replenishing the earth, and subduing the forces of darkness (Genesis 1:28; Mark 16:15-18; Ephesians 3:10).

So what do we call this restored church? Some have labeled it the Organic Church, others are calling it the Simple Church, and then there are the House Church proponents. There are other names, but these are the most common. Let's see if we can get a hint from the Word of God.

> *And I say also unto thee, That thou art Peter, and upon this rock I will build my church... (Matthew 16:18)*

*Praising God, and having favour with all the people. And the Lord added to the church ...( Acts 2:47)*

*And God hath set some in the church...( 1Corinthians 12:28)*

*Is any sick among you? let him call for the elders of the church... (James 5:14)*

*I wrote unto the church...( 3John 1:9)*

I understand the reason for the adjectives (organic, simple, house) defining a particular type of church, but in my opinion, they have the potential of creating new sects in the Body of Christ. These monikers have the same impact as calling a church Baptist, Methodist or Pentecostal. Labels inadvertently and sometimes willfully separate us. God forbid that this would evolve into a day when the organic church folks are at odds with the simple church folks, and the house church folks are snubbing them both (1Corinthians 1:10-13).

Jesus said He would build His Church. The apostles called it the church, the church of God (1Corinthians 1:2), and the whole church (Romans 16:23). So as mundane as it may seem to some, I simply call the church what it is called in scripture – the church.

I have attempted to avoid using terms like house, simple or organic to describe the church. In some places the term house church is used to stress a certain point. At the end of the day, I simply see the church as – the church.

In defense of the organic, simple and house church proponents, I understand that the church is organic in nature, simple in application and that meeting in the house is the most biblical method of gathering. My belief is not to refute or diminish the contribution of the Holy Spirit's work through them. Much of what reinforced my revelation came from their books. However, I pray that in the seasons ahead we will see *the church* as *the church* – plain and simple.

God has given me a revelation and an assignment. The revelation is an understanding of New Testament church structure. My assignment is to plant regional churches that reflect that structure – beginning with my local fellowship

## FOR I NEITHER RECEIVED IT OF MAN...

*...neither was I taught it, but by the revelation of Jesus Christ. (Galatians 1:12)*

Before I began my study of church structure, the Holy Spirit had began painting a picture in my spirit that contrasted where the church is today against what it should be.

It was a picture that began on a blank canvas in my spirit. I could see it, yet I had no capacity to touch it. I knew what I was looking at, yet I found it impossible to clearly articulate what I saw. I knew the reality of what I could see, yet it has taken over fifteen years to find an entrance and begin moving towards it.

Dr. Bill Hamon says that, "When something is born of God within a person, there is no option but to stick with it. The way of the Lord must be found and implemented for the vision to be fulfilled throughout Christendom.[1]

## A Revelation and an Assignment

In the mid-1980's the Lord told me that I would be a *'part of the apostolic renewal'*. I had no clue what this meant. My paradigm of *apostolic* was a particular denomination – not church structure.

Over the years, the Holy Spirit gently introduced me to various truths in the Word of God. First it was my understanding of the Kingdom of God. Then it was the apostolic, prophetic and five-fold ministry gifts. This brought me to the place where I could see the biblical church structure in comparison to what we generally practice today. This revelation continued as the Lord gently kept highlighting areas of church practice that seem to conflict with scriptural truth.

God has given me a revelation and an assignment. The revelation is an understanding of New Testament church structure. My assignment is to plant regional churches that reflect that structure – beginning with my local fellowship.

It is my belief that God desires for the first century structure to be available to all church systems – not just the organic, simple and house church groups. God has made it clear to me that any *'move'* of His is not limited to special interest groups. Every believer must have the opportunity to participate. My assignment is to establish a prototype church that transitions from the current church model we know to a New Testament model.

I have become more empathetic to Noah (Hebrews 11:7). He spent years building a structure he had never seen for a time he had never been in. Imagine how difficult it was for him to describe his building project. My goal in this book is to describe to you what I see in my spirit – a church unlike any I have ever seen, or participated in. Yet, it is a church that I believe reflects the heart of the Father.

> *And to make all men see what is the fellowship of the mystery, which from the beginning of the world hath been hid in God, who created all things by Jesus Christ: To the intent that now unto the principalities and powers in heavenly places might be known by the church the manifold wisdom of God, According to the eternal purpose which he purposed in Christ Jesus our Lord: (Ephesians 3:9-11)*

The Lord is still building His Church – in the twenty-first century. His Church will accomplish His purposes in the earth. It will be a church that is solely directed by the Holy Spirit, yet it will be guided by those entrusted by the Father to oversee His purposes. In my spirit I see a Glorious Church that is gentle enough to win and disciple the vilest of sinners, and strong enough to subdue the darkest forces of hell. I see the Lord's Church existing – His way. I see a Church completely void of meaningless programs, time wasting events and human interference, but rather a Church that is filled with the presence of God Himself in the earth.

## THE CHANGING STRUCTURE

The majority of churches that exist today are organized spiritual business entities. They operate similarly to corporate America. There is a CEO, or Sr. Pastor. There is a Board of Directors, probably elders or deacons. There is a staff—either paid or volunteer. There are the customers—namely the lay people who come each week to financially underwrite the corporation/church. And finally, there is the product—their version of the gospel and its presentation. I personally shudder at using the term 'product' for the gospel, but in many churches that is what it has been reduced to.

Most church leaders will acknowledge that the government of the church is a theocracy, yet they worship in churches whose governmental structure resembles Roberts Rules of Order more than scripture. They depend upon one man to lead them rather than ministering to each other under the guidance of a plurality of elders. Rather than biblical consensus for decision making, they campaign for votes and are often led by dominant personalities rather than the Holy Spirit.

The spirit driving most of these 'corporation/churches' is self preservation. They devise methods, practices and policies necessary to maintain their survival. Unfortunately, many of these policies have no scriptural merit, and they are practiced at the expense of the very ones they are called to serve.

## WHY THE CHANGE?

The church ceased to expand aggressively when it left the simplicity of gathering in homes and one-on-one discipling. The church structure became a sterile monolithic entity that no longer saw the Kingdom of God as its focus. The believer became a spectator void of any authority and relevance other than to 'amen' the leadership and financially underwrite their goals. This structure was birthed in the third century and has become religious tradition ever since (Mark 7:13). The Holy Spirit is calling us back to the simplicity of first century church, because an accurate church structure underpins the expansion of the Kingdom of God in the earth.

The structural restoration this book espouses is to return the church to her first century glory. It is restoring first century values, principles and practices to the twenty-first century church. It is a church where a plurality of elders will oversee, guide and protect the church in a city or region. It is a church where five-fold ministers skillfully equip saints to perpetuate the maturing and growth of the church. And mostly, this restored structure will release millions of believers into the earth as disciples of the Lord Jesus Christ, who in turn will make millions of more disciples (Matthew 28:19-20).

In returning to first century *practices*, believers will meet in their homes to encourage and build one another. In returning to *values*, believers will follow apostolic doctrine and literally live out the fifty or more 'one another' scriptures in the Word of God. This is a reflection of the church in the New Testament expressed in contemporary times.

# The Definition, The Values and the Kingdom Mandate

**4**

There are three things you must first learn in No Longer Church As Usual; (1) *definition of the church*, (2) *the values of the church* and (3) the *Kingdom Mandate*. It is important that you do not confuse the *definition* of the church with the *values* or the *Kingdom Mandate*. They are clearly intertwined, yet they are each distinct and should be understood separately.

The *definition* of the New Testament Church reveals *what* the church is. It is the immediate picture that comes to mind when the word 'church' is mentioned. The definition readily identifies the church by those who view her. It describes what she is, more than what she does.

The *values* reveal the culture of the church. Paul taught that we speak the same thing, and that we be of the same mind and judgment (1Corinthians 1:10). As the church embraces the same values, the strength of the church will be seen by the world. The values existed long before denominational doctrine, which has in many cases diluted the values. New Testament values are the foundation from which doctrine is built.

The *Kingdom Mandate* is the divine mission of the Church. It is the marching orders for the church. It is the purpose established in the heart of God from the beginning. It is not an alternative plan—it is the plan. Every act of the Church must be in concert with the divine mission.

The combination of the definition, values and Kingdom Mandate helps to clarify our understanding of the New Testament Church. Let's now look at the definition.


## THE DEFINITION

The New Testament Church is an assembly of believers, committed to the Kingdom Mandate, who gather one or more times each week under the Headship of Jesus Christ; who are submitted to each other in love; who support each other's on-going work of being and making disciples of the Lord Jesus Christ; who edify, exhort and comfort one another; who submit and relate to elders, ministry gifts and apostolic leaders; who participate in planting and supporting new assemblies of believers to do the same with their prayers, time, finances and material resources.

I have had the opportunity to share this definition (all ninety-two words of it) with several leaders around the country. They all agree that this is a very comprehensive definition and that removing any portion drastically changes what is being expressed. There are eight components found in the definition. Let's discuss each one.

## (1) The New Testament Church is an assembly of believers...

We must be clear in our definition of New Testament. The Gospels reveal that Jesus taught that He did not come to destroy the law, but rather that He came to fulfill it (Matthew 5:17,21-33). Jesus regularly drew upon Old Testament text. Compare Matthew 4:4 with Deuteronomy 8:3. Compare Luke 4:18-19 to Isaiah 61:1-3.

A New Testament church models the values, principles and practices that were taught and demonstrated by Jesus Christ, the founding apostles and the first century believers. The New Testament books are a record of these pioneers living out their revelation of Jesus Christ through Old Testament text. What we know as the New Testament books did not exist during their lifetime.

Immediately after Christ ascension, it is clear that the apostles drew from Old Testament writings to teach, make decisions and to explain their activities (Acts 1:20; 2:16-18; 24:14; 28:23). Apostles Paul, James and John relied on Old Testament text to teach and bring correction (Romans 10:5; 1Corinthian 9:9; 2Corinthians 3:7; James 2:8-12; 1John 3:4).

The book of Hebrews outlines superiority of the New Covenant over the old, but does not eliminate the old as a foundation (Hebrews 7:19-28; 8:7; 12:24).

Embracing the New Testament is not at the exclusion of the Old Testament. We rely on both the Old and New Testament. The entire canon of scripture from Genesis to Revelation is our written guide for doctrine, reproof, correction and instruction in righteousness (2Timothy 3:16). As New Testament believers we have no authority to eliminate or add to what has been written in the sixty-six books of the bible (Revelation 22:19).

The word *church* is translated from the Greek word *ecclesia*. The basic meaning is '*a calling out or an assembly*'. Throughout the New Testament, every use of the word church implies an assembly of believers. However, the word *church* was not originally a 'Christian' term.

> In the same way that the Roman *ecclesia* was to ensure the policies of the governor of Rome were enacted, the Lord's *ecclesia* (church) is the only arm of the Kingdom of God that is to ensure that the policies and decrees of heaven are enacted and enforced in the earth

*When Jesus came into the coasts of Caesarea Philippi, he asked his disciples, saying, Whom do men say that I the Son of man am? And they said, Some say that thou art John the Baptist: some, Elias; and others, Jeremias, or one of the prophets. He saith unto them, But whom say ye that I am? And Simon Peter answered and said, Thou art the Christ, the Son of the living God. And Jesus answered and said unto him, Blessed art thou, Simon Barjona: for flesh and blood hath not revealed it unto thee, but my Father which is in heaven. And I say also unto thee, That thou art Peter, and upon this rock I will build my church; and the gates of hell shall not prevail against it (Matthew 16:13-18)*

This common passage is often quoted to express the truth

that Jesus alone is building His Church. But when you read this passage did you note that Jesus did not take the time to define what a 'church' was to His disciples? He simply said that He would build His Church and there is no indication that the disciples failed to understand what He meant.

In the book of Daniel, it was prophesied that God would establish a kingdom that would never be destroyed; a kingdom that was hewn out of a mountain without hands and capable of overcoming all other kingdoms. This evolved through four empires. The first three as identified by biblical historians are the Chaldean (head of gold), the Medes and Persians (breast and arms of silver), and the Grecian (belly and thighs of brass). The fourth was the Roman Empire (legs and feet of iron). It is the Roman Empire that existed during the time of Jesus Christ (Daniel 2:31-45).

The Romans were more civil than the first three empires when they conquered new territory. Yet, there was never any doubt that you were under Roman jurisdiction. The Romans had borrowed some of the methodologies of the Greeks, including the concept of *'a called out assembly'* or *ecclesia*. *Ecclesia* is the Greek word that is translated into English as *church*.

The *ecclesia* was an arm of the Roman government that helped to oversee and manage the policies of Rome in a territory. Whatever Rome desired would be taught and enforced by the *ecclesia*. The *ecclesia* was known by the disciples and to the people of Jesus' day as an arm of the government.

This historical understanding of the word *ecclesia* is the first step to opening our understanding of what the church is. The Roman model of *ecclesia* that Jesus chose, gives us insight to the purpose of the Church in the New Testament. In the same way that the Roman *ecclesia* was to ensure the policies of the governor of Rome were enacted, the Lord's *ecclesia* (church) is the only arm of the Kingdom of God that is to ensure that the policies and decrees of heaven are enacted and enforced in the earth.

## (2) committed to the Kingdom Mandate...

The Kingdom Mandate is the mission of the church. It is the mission God had in mind for the Church from the foundation of the world. The church must continually and systematically recapture the territory stolen by the devil. That is its assignment. The Kingdoms of religion, government, entertainment, media, business, education and family must be regained and made subject to the Lord (Revelation 11:15).

In the Garden of Eden, man was given a mandate. Whether you see it as a divine assignment or an eternal mission, this mandate will guide every church towards God's ultimate purpose – which is to establish His Kingdom in the earth (Matthew 24:14; 1Corinthians 15:24; Revelation 11:15). The Kingdom Mandate, as it is called, is to be *fruitful, multiply, replenish and subdue and have dominion* (Genesis 1:26-28).

The Kingdom Mandate was given to man before they fell into sin. No where in scripture was this mandate ever revoked. In fact, Jesus, the apostles and the first century church seem to reinforce this fact (Mark 6:12-13: John 15:16; Acts 5:14; 9:31). The Kingdom Mandate is part of the church's definition because it gives purpose for the assembly of believers. Every assembly or *ecclesia* must be fully committed to Kingdom Mandate and its completion in the earth.

## (3) who gather one or more times each week under the Headship of Jesus Christ;

The church is an assembly of believers. These believers become family. You cannot mandate when a family gathers. They simply gather. But when this family gathers, everyone acknowledges that Jesus Christ is the sole head. Those considered leaders among them are only such because of their submission to Jesus Christ. Their authority is not hierarchal in nature, but rather rooted in submission to the Lordship of Jesus Christ and to each other. It is authority that emanates from revelation. Every believer knows they are a king and priest, but they understand that their authority only goes as far as their obedience to Jesus Christ.

Gathering in one place at least once each week is to reinforce the covenant relationship of the family. The weekly gathering is similar to a family get together where everyone brings something to share with the other family members. Whether it be a meal, a word of encouragement, a revelation, a song, or even financial gifts, a family gathers to encourage and build one another (1Corinthians 14:26; Hebrews 10:25). Family members are in contact with each other on a daily basis. Family members care for each other daily.

**(4) who are submitted to each other in love;**
Of all the 'one-anothers' in scripture, the command to love one another shows up the most. Our willingness to submit to each other in love creates an atmosphere for the Holy Spirit to work.

> *Beloved, if God so loved us, we ought also to love one another. No man hath seen God at any time. If we love one another, God dwelleth in us, and his love is perfected in us. (1John 4:11-12)*

> *Herein is our love made perfect, that we may have boldness in the day of judgment: because as he is, so are we in this world. There is no fear in love; but perfect love casteth out fear: because fear hath torment. He*

*that feareth is not made perfect in love. (1John 4:17-18)*

In his epistles, John describes a love that is perfected. The Greek word from which perfected is translated throughout these scriptures is the verb *teleioo*, which means *to bring to an end by completing*. Love, John states, is brought to completion through our interaction with each other. If we love one another, God's love is brought to completion in us.

To paraphrase verse 17, John says that "this is how our love is completed". He goes on to say that this complete love eradicates fear, and that fear is proof that we are not yet completed in love. All of this is predicated on our relationships with our brothers and sisters (1John 4:7).

This complete fearless love can only exist among believers who are in covenant relationship with each other. This does not mean that believers are without faults. It simply means that a love that is being completed in one believer can find fellowship with other believers without condemning or being judgmental (1Peter 4:8).

**(5) who support each other's on-going work of being and making disciples of the Lord Jesus Christ;**
Jesus made the requirements of becoming a disciple crystal clear. Anyone who does not deny himself, take up his cross daily and follow Jesus, cannot be His disciple (Luke 9:23). Anyone who does not give up all that he has cannot be His disciple (Luke 14:33). The price of becoming a disciple is high.

Making disciples is also the process by which sinners are transformed by the saving grace of Jesus Christ. We are commanded by Jesus to make disciples of all nations (Matthew 28:19). This may seem like a daunting task when each of us personally struggle with the concept of self–denial. How can you make someone something that you personally struggle with becoming?

> *And I myself also am persuaded of you, my brethren, that ye also are full of goodness, filled with all knowledge, able also to admonish one another. (Romans 15:14)*

> *And let us consider one another to provoke unto love and to good works: Not forsaking the assembling of ourselves together, as the manner of some is; but exhorting one another: and so much the more, as ye see the day approaching. (Hebrews 10:24-25)*

Once again *'one-anothering'* comes into play. Paul wrote the Roman Christians about their ability to admonish one another. In Hebrews, the author encouraged the believers to provoke one another to good works and to exhort each other when they regularly assembled.

This exposes one of the mystical strengths of the New Testament Church structure. It is during the face to face, living room interaction that believers are encouraged and strengthened. The greatest paradigm shift is to understand that believers grow spiritually from a combination of close interaction with each other, followed by spiritual input from ministry gifts and the corporate gatherings.

God desires a family who loves, encourages and strengthen one another. The auditorium like atmosphere of most churches, regardless of size, implicitly discourages this level of interaction among the saints. There more fellowship and interaction after church in the lobby than during the time when the formal service is underway. Believers leave these settings often carrying the same burdens they came with.

In the New Testament Church, we bear one another's burden to the point of feeling each others pain, embracing one another's sorrows and sharing one another's joys (1Corinthians 12:25-26). This is how disciples are developed. Disciples are made through personal interaction.

**(6) who edify, exhort and comfort one another;**
We should always desire the best for each other (Philippians 2:3). As our love matures for each other, we have more capacity to speak correction, direction and protection into the lives of our brothers and sisters. Likewise, the same mature love will cause us to receive the correction, direction and protection from our bothers and sisters. The bible teaches us to speak the truth in love (Ephesians 4:15,25). This only serves to make us better in our walk with the Lord.

Edification, exhortation and comforting are all attributes of prophecy (1Corinthians 14:3). Prophecy edifies or builds the church. When we prophesy to each other, it brings strength to the church. It builds a spiritual camaraderie that can endure tough times and difficult situations. As New Testament believers, we must strive to create an atmosphere that continually builds those we are in covenant with.

**(7) who submit and relate to elders, ministry gifts and apostolic leaders;**
We need not fear using the biblical terminology of 'submission'. A healthy New Testament Church will submit to accurate leadership without fail. Leadership who serve the church as Jesus and the apostles did carry the responsibility of having others submit to them. However, true leaders do not relish having others submit to them. They recognize that they also must submit to someone. (Romans 12:10; 13:1; Ephesians 5:21; 1Peter 5:5). A true leader's focus is the greater purposes of the Father, not their own perceived authority.

The heart of the church is found in voluntary submission to authority. The bible teaches to *'obey them that have rule over you'* (Hebrews 13:17). The Greek word *peitho* that was translated to *obey* in this passage has the implication of one having confidence in another. Submission to leadership is by choice not coercion. We submit because we have confidence in those who lead us.

In chapters seven through ten, 21$^{st}$ century leadership is discussed in greater detail. I pray you will see leadership as it is meant to be. I believe you will see the strength accurate leadership will help to produce in the church.

**(8)who participate in planting and supporting new assemblies of believers to do the same with their prayers, time, finances and material resources.**

The common theme that flows throughout the New Testament church is 'one-anothering'. We love one another. We edify one another. We exhort one another and the list goes on. Another theme is the commitment to the Kingdom Mandate. The spiritual DNA of every member demands that we continue to multiply ourselves throughout the earth. To that end, no ecclesia is fully complete until it has helped to give birth to another ecclesia. Therefore, every gathering should willingly give spiritual, financial and human resources into planting new churches and helping them to become healthy.

> The New Testament Church is an assembly of believers, committed to the Kingdom Mandate, who gather one or more times each week under the Headship of Jesus Christ; who are submitted to each other in love; who support each other's on-going work of being and making disciples of the

Lord Jesus Christ; who edify, exhort and comfort one another; who submit and relate to elders, ministry gifts and apostolic leaders; who participate in planting and supporting new assemblies of believers to do the same with their prayers, time, finances and material resources.

This describes a vibrant living church (Ephesians 2:21-22). This defines the glorious Church for which Jesus shed his blood (Acts 20:28). This is the church Jesus said He would build (Matthew 16:18). This is the church through which principalities and powers will learn the eternal wisdom of God (Ephesians 3:10-11). Is this the church you want to be a part of? I believe it is. Let's learn some more.

# The Structure of the Church   5

Church structure is not a doctrine. The first century church did not consider the way they met and worshipped a doctrinal issue. Yet, it was their lifestyle and tradition. It appears that the New Testament writers assumed their readers understood the structure. The believers simply gathered from house to house.

Because gathering methods are not a doctrine, some assume that how we meet is insignificant. But as you will see, our method of meeting has tremendous impact on the purposes of the Lord in the earth. Historically, how we meet today did not begin until around 312 AD. When this system of worship began, it took the ministry out of the hands of the people, and put it into the hands of professional clergy.

The restoration of church structure is to release the saints for the work of the ministry, and to fulfill the purposes of God in the earth. The transition is not just to move from 'big building church' to 'house church', but it is a move to lay the groundwork for the saints of God to do the work of ministry. As the Holy Spirit emphasizes the saints doing the 'work of ministry', the way we gather will be a natural outcome.

The most recent move of God has been the restoration of the ministry gifts – apostles, prophets, evangelist, pastors and teachers. Like many previous moves of God, people tend to gravitate and camp in a particular arena. This results in factions that are apostolic, prophetic, evangelical, etc. This is wrong.

> *And he gave some, apostles; and some, prophets; and some, evangelists; and some, pastors and teachers; <u>For the perfecting of the saints, for the work of the ministry, for the edifying of the body of Christ</u> (Ephesians 4:11-12)*

The ministry gifts were given by Jesus Christ to His church for a specific purpose – to perfect or mature the saints for the work of ministry. The role of ministry gifts is not to control but rather mentor the saints. The work of ministry itself is to be done by the saints.

Beginning around 1990 the ministry of the 21ˢᵗ Century apostle began developing. Unfortunately many have tried to make the apostolic role fit into the institutional church structure. Some modern day apostles seem to find fulfillment within their apostolic networks. Their spiritual worth is often measured by the number of churches they have 'under' them. But that is simply the same old hierarchal method being done under an apostolic banner.

The Apostle Paul planted several churches but there is no

evidence that these churches were 'under' him. In fact, after he organized a church he stayed in contact with them but turned the responsibility of the oversight to elders. I believe his final salutation to the elders in Ephesus gives us a glimpse of his heart.

> *Take heed therefore unto yourselves, and to all the flock, over the which the Holy Ghost hath made you overseers, to feed the church of God, which he hath purchased with his own blood (Acts 20:28).*

> *And now, brethren, I commend you to God, and to the word of his grace, which is able to build you up, and to give you an inheritance among all them which are sanctified (Acts 20:32).*

Paul clearly saw the value of local churches being governed by local eldership. He did not feel the need to 'be there' and always hold their hands.

## AN INCOMPLETE MESSAGE

> *And a certain Jew named Apollos, born at Alexandria, an eloquent man, and mighty in the scriptures, came to Ephesus. This man was instructed in the way of the Lord; and being fervent in the spirit, he spake and taught diligently the things of the Lord, knowing only the baptism of John. And he began to speak boldly in the synagogue: whom when Aquila and Priscilla had heard, they took him unto them, and expounded unto him the way of God more perfectly (Acts 18:24-26).*

When Priscilla and Acquila came upon Apollos, it was obvious that he was eloquent in his teaching of the baptism of John. They did not publicly demean or debate him. Instead they took him aside and taught him the way of God more perfectly. The message Apollos preached was not wrong, it was simply incomplete. Likewise, the way we commonly do church is not totally wrong, it is incomplete.

## THE COMPLETE CHURCH

There are three things that complete the church – the *presence* of Christ, the *power* of Christ and the *purpose* of Christ. These three are expressed in *the church meeting in houses, the whole church and the temple.* They create a three-fold cord that constitutes the structure necessary to release God's people in the earth.

The *presence* of Christ is experienced in the small intimate setting of the house church. It is when two or three are gathered together that Jesus declares He is in their midst (Matthew 18:20). The *power* of Christ is experienced in the collective gathering of the whole church.

When the first whole church meeting took place in the upper room, the Holy Ghost fell on all of them (Acts 2:4). It was the multitude of believers that created an atmosphere where the apostles were empowered, grace was experienced and no one lacked (Acts 4:32-34).

The *purpose* of Christ is discovered in the temple. Yes, our body is the temple of the Holy Ghost (1 Corinthians 3:16). As the living temple of the Lord, the indwelling Holy Ghost teaches us all things (John 14:26). However, it was in the *physical* brick and mortar temple and synagogues where prayers were made and many believing Jews were taught (Acts 3:1; 5:21).

## THE CHURCH IN THE HOUSE OF...

There is no teaching in scripture specifically relating to house churches. You won't find a scripture that says, "thou shalt meet in houses". We must look carefully into the Word of God to understand the magnitude and importance of the house church.

*Likewise greet the church that is in their (Priscilla and Aquila) house (Romans 16:5a)*

*The churches of Asia salute you. Aquila and Priscilla salute you much in the Lord, <u>with the church that is in their house</u> (1 Corinthians 16:19)*

*Salute the brethren which are in Laodicea, and Nymphas, and <u>the church which is in his house</u> (Colossians 4:15)*

*And to our beloved Apphia, and Archippus our fellowsoldier, <u>and to the church in thy house</u> (Philemon 1:2)*

The above passages all show that there were churches meeting in the houses of Priscilla and Aquila, Nymphas and Philemon. These were individuals with whom Paul had direct communication and fellowship. The fact that they were the only ones mentioned by name, does not imply that there were not other house churches.

Jason's House

*But the Jews which believed not, moved with envy, took unto them certain lewd fellows of the baser sort, and gathered a company, and set all the city on an uproar, <u>and assaulted the house of Jason</u>, and sought to bring them out to the people. And when they found them not, they drew Jason and certain brethren unto the rulers of the city, crying, <u>These that have turned the world upside down are come hither also; Whom Jason hath received</u>: and these all do contrary to the decrees of Caesar, saying that there is another king, one Jesus. And they troubled the people and* *the rulers of the city, when they heard these things. And when they had taken security of Jason, and of the other, they let them go (Acts 17:5-9).*

In an attempt to stop the message of the Gospel, the Jews consorted with low class individuals to attack believers. Where did they attack? The church in the house – specifically the house of Jason.

Some scholars believe that Jason was a relative of Paul (Romans 16:21), and therefore conclude that it was in Jason's home that Paul and Silas stayed while they were in Thessalonica. I believe that when in his home, Paul and Silas continued to teach the Gospel of the Kingdom. This was a pattern he had wherever he went. Therefore it is highly probable that he ministered from Jason's house.

<u>Paul taught from house to house...</u>
Paul encouraged the elders in Ephesus and made it clear that he taught them publicly and in houses.

*And from Miletus he sent to Ephesus, and called the elders of the church. And when they were come to him, he said unto them, Ye know, from the first day that I came into Asia, after what manner I have been with you at all seasons, Serving the Lord with all humility of mind, and with many tears, and temptations, which befell me by the lying in wait of the Jews: And how I kept back nothing that was profitable unto you, but have shewed you, <u>and have taught you publickly, and from house to house</u> (Acts 20:17-20)*

<u>Lydia's House</u>
What about the house of Lydia? Was there a church in her house? There is no definitive scripture that will answer yes, yet a closer look greatly implies the possibility.

*And when it was day, the magistrates sent the serjeants, saying, Let those men go. And the keeper of the prison told this saying to Paul, The magistrates have sent to let you go: now therefore depart, and go in peace. But Paul said unto them, They have beaten us openly uncondemned, being Romans, and have cast us into prison; and now do they thrust us out privily? nay verily; but let them come themselves and fetch us out. And the serjeants told these words unto the magistrates: and they feared, when they heard that they were Romans. And they came and besought them, and brought them out, and desired them to depart out of the city. And they went out of the prison, and entered into the house of Lydia: and when they had seen the brethren, they comforted them, and departed (Acts 16:35-40).*

After Paul and Silas were released from prison, they went to the house of Lydia. It was there that they met the brethren, possibly the local elders, and was comforted by them. Why were the brethren in Lydia's house? Could it be that this was a common meeting place for Christians? This seems to be the conclusion found in the Robertson's New Testament Word Pictures Commentary.

Into the house of Lydia (pros tên Ludian). No word in the Greek for "house," but it means the house of Lydia. Note "the brethren" here, not merely Luke and Timothy, but other brethren now converted besides those in the house of the jailor. The four missionaries were guests of Lydia (verse Ac 16:15) and probably the church now met in her home.[2]

Saul attacked churches in local houses...

Before Paul's conversion, he was an enemy of the church. In today's vernacular, he was literally licensed by the high priest (Acts 9:1). With the authority he had from the Jewish leadership he aggressively went forth looking for those who followed Jesus Christ. Where did he look? Again, scripture makes it clear.

> *As for Saul, he made havock of the church, <u>entering into every house</u>, and haling men and women committed them to prison (Acts 8:3).*

Once again we see where the saints were most likely to be found – in the house church. Notice that Saul entered into *every house*, which implies that there were many house churches for him to choose from. The fact that Saul could easily find houses where saints met dispels the idea that the believers met in homes to avoid persecution.

From these passages it is obvious that the house church played a major role in the first century church.

## WHAT DID THEY DO?

The next question we need to address is what the saints did in these house churches to experience the presence of Christ? We will find the answer to this question scattered throughout the entire New Testament.

> *And they, continuing daily with one accord in the temple, and <u>breaking bread from house to house</u>, did eat their meat with gladness and singleness of heart (Acts 2:46)*

The first thing we see the saints doing is breaking bread. I believe this could include sharing a meal together and also the celebration of the Lord's Supper. Anytime the saints shared a meal there was a vivid reminder of life of Christ (1Corinthians 11:26).

In my studies of cell churches, the idea of an ice breaker is often suggested. This may be good, but nothing beats sharing a meal with friends. Even more, those who regularly share in the Lord's Supper together in a small intimate setting will generally not need ice breakers to open their meetings.

> For where two or three are gathered together in my name, there am I in the midst of them. (Matthw 18:20)

> Not forsaking the assembling of ourselves together, as the manner of some is; but exhorting one another: and so much the more, as ye see the day approaching. (Hebrews 10:25)

The above passages give us an understanding of the *presence* of Christ that is found in the house church setting. Jesus said where two or three are gathered in His name, He would be in the midst of them. How does this happen?

> Even the mystery which hath been hid from ages and from generations, but now is made manifest to his saints: To whom God would make known what is the riches of the glory of this mystery among the Gentiles; which is <u>Christ in you, the hope of glory</u>: (Colossians 1:26-27)

> Ye are our epistle written in our hearts, known and read of all men: <u>Forasmuch as ye are manifestly declared to be the epistle of Christ</u> ministered by us, written not with ink, but with the Spirit of the living God; not in tables of stone, but in fleshy tables of the heart. (2Corinthians 3:2-3)

The eternal plan of God is that each of us would be a reflection of Christ in the earth. When believers gather, each person is an expression of Christ. Everyone in the group is strengthened and encouraged, to rise to new levels of maturity (Ephesians 4:16-17).

When we gather together with other believers we become the church in its most basic form. It is in the small intimate gatherings that Christ promises to be in the midst. Christ in me connects with Christ in you, and Christ in us becomes greater than our individual experiences in Christ. We all are edified and strengthened by His presence in us and among us.

Matthew 18:20 should not be quoted as an apologetic response to a small crowd showing up to what was expected to be a large corporate meeting. Jesus meant exactly what He said when He suggested two or three gathering. He was encouraging the small intimate gathering of saints. It is only in the small setting of the house churches that the full understanding of *"I am in the midst"* can truly be experienced. It is there we experience the *presence* of Christ.

## THE POWER OF CHRIST IN THE WHOLE CHURCH

The *presence* of Christ is experienced in the house church gatherings and the *power* of Christ is experienced in the corporate gatherings or the whole church.

> *Then pleased it the apostles and elders, <u>with the whole church</u>, to send chosen men of their own company to Antioch with Paul and Barnabas; [namely], Judas surnamed Barsabas, and Silas, chief men among the brethren:( Acts 15:22)*

> *Gaius mine host, and <u>of the whole church</u>, saluteth you... (Romans 16:23)*

> *If therefore <u>the whole church be come together</u> into one place, and all speak with tongues, and there come in [those that are] unlearned, or unbelievers, will they not say that ye are mad?(1Corinthians 14:23)*

Those who gather in houses run the risk of becoming isolated from other believers. It is wrong for believers to purposely disconnect themselves from other Christians and refuse any input from proven spiritual authority. Such groups often become in-grown and biblically dysfunctional. For the sake of accountability, house churches should at least be connected with other house churches within a city. When they all come together, they collectively form the *whole church*.

> For as the body is one, and hath many members, and all the members of that one body, being many, are one body: so also is Christ. (1 Corinthians 12:12)

> But now [are they] many members, yet but one body. (1 Corinthians 12:20)

The first purpose of the whole church gathering is vision. It is necessary for every believer to regularly see that they belong to something greater than themselves. It is important that they realize their house church gathering is part of the larger Body of Christ.

Elijah had a pity party and complained that he was alone in his righteous efforts. God had to remind him that there were seven thousand who had not bowed to Baal (1Kings 19:18). Elijah's problem stemmed from his temporary withdrawal from others by hiding in a cave (1Kings 19:9). Whenever you cut yourself from other people, your spiritual perception of yourself will become blurred and very often erroneous.

Here is my point. In the whole church setting, believers can worship and interact with other house church members and leaders. Those praying about leadership can be encouraged by existing leaders. Existing leaders can network with other leaders in matters that can edify their gatherings. There is power gained in the corporate gatherings.

## ONENESS AND CONTINUITY

The second purpose of the whole church gathering is oneness and continuity.

Paul encouraged the Corinthian believers to all speak the same thing, destroy divisions among them, and to be perfectly joined together in the same mind and in the same judgment (1Corinthians 1:10). The first century church continued steadfastly in the Apostles doctrine (Acts 2:42).

The church was birthed after it was reported that the believers were in *one accord in one place* (Acts 2:1). After the entrance of the Holy Spirit several times their 'oneness' was expressed in scripture.

*And all that believed were together, and had all things common (Acts 2:44)*

*And they, continuing daily with one accord in the temple, and breaking bread from house to house, did eat their meat with gladness and singleness of heart (Acts 2:46)*

*... they lifted up their voice to God with one accord...(Acts 4:24)*

*And the multitude of them that believed were of one heart and of one soul: neither said any of them that ought of the things which he possessed was his own; but they had all things common (Acts 4:32)*

The result of their oneness was mind blowing. Scripture says, "*...with great power gave the apostles witness of the resurrection of the Lord Jesus: and great grace was upon them all. Neither was there any among them that lacked...*"(Ac 4:33-34a). In other words, there was clear strength as they saw and functioned as one.

## CELEBRATION

The third purpose of the whole church is *celebration*. There are no substitutes for corporate praise and worship. It causes the most timid believers to draw closer to the Lord. It often encourages believers to enter into deeper levels of adoration.

Multi-level business proponents have learned the value of the 'whole church principle'. Of course they don't call it that, but they clearly employ the principles of the house and whole church. Here's how.

You receive a call from someone inviting you to a small meeting where a business opportunity will be discussed. At this meeting you are 'sold' the benefits of this opportunity in relationship to your personal dreams and aspirations. You get excited, pay your entry fee and join up. For weeks you continue to meet with your small group learning how to get their fool-proof system to work for you. Then your up-line (mentor) invites you to a regional gathering held in another city and you agree to attend.

When you arrive at the large meeting there are thousands of people gathered. "Wow!" you think to yourself, "Are all these people in this business, too?" When the program begins, the music is fun and exciting, the success testimonies are inspiring, and the vision for your possible success is made clearer to you. The *"you can make it-you can succeed"* atmosphere of the meeting charges your spirit to keep pursuing your dreams.

Can you see what has taken place? You gathered with hundreds, possible thousands of like minded people. Your personal involvement began the same as the person you sat next to. Your city, state, and small group may differ, but your involvement was only differentiated by location.

Each of you have your own individual needs and aspirations. Your dreams are found within the larger corporate vision. You go home knowing that you are a part of something big and powerful. This is the power of the whole church meeting.

The majority of believers are familiar with the traditional church setting. They are very similar to whole church gatherings. The problem is that in the traditional setting, two conflicting components try to co-exist. They are the presence of Christ only found in the intimate small gatherings, and the power of Christ experienced in the corporate gathering.

The house church is divinely designed to include the participation of every member. The whole church is not designed for everyone to participate. The house church fosters *covenant*, while the whole church promotes *connection*. The house church is an expression of the *individual*, the whole church is an expression of the *body*. The house church is '*lively stones*', whereas the whole church is a '*spiritual house*' (1Peter 2:5). The house church is the *unseen foundation*, and the whole church is the *visible building* seen by the world.

## THE END OF THE 80/20 RULE

The restoration of first century church structure is to release the saints for the work of ministry.

It is commonly known that twenty percent of the people do eighty percent of the work in traditional churches. Programs are invented to get more involvement, but usually the same people are involved in most of these programs. The culprit is the structure of the church – not the people. Ministry has been minimized to ushering, singing in the choir, board membership or volunteering in one of many programs. We have created congregations of well meaning 'human-doings' rather than spirit filled 'human beings'.

The auditorium style worship services send an implicit message to most believers that they are only spectators. Fellowship and interaction is limited time spent in the lobby before or after the worship service. For the most part, you just sit and look over the back of the head of the person in front of you and watch the 'religious performance.' The auditorium style setting is only conducive to whole church gatherings when personal interaction is designed to be limited.

As the Church grows and progresses, it is important that we keep the differences between the church that gathers in the house and whole church clear. In the house church there is *personal participation*. In the whole church there is *corporate impartation*.

## THE TEMPLE: THE PURPOSE OF CHRIST

In the house church we experience the *presence* of Christ. In the whole church we experience the *power* of Christ. Between the two is the temple where we pursue the *purpose* of Christ.

> *And they continued stedfastly in the apostles' doctrine and fellowship, and in breaking of bread, and in prayers. (Acts 2:42)*

A friend of mine once said that, "Doctrine is what we view, and what we view is what we do!" The church has been gravely divided by satan over doctrinal issues. We camp around our pet doctrines and defend them against those who would dare oppose us.

Admittedly, one of my fears is that what is taught in NO LONGER CHURCH AS USUAL will be reduced to unwritten doctrine that divides us further into opposing camps. This danger can be accentuated when we find ourselves preaching 'it' (church structure) rather than 'Him', Jesus Christ. Jesus said, if He were lifted up, all men would be drawn to Him (John 12:32).

The preaching of our programs, events or movements can potentially divide the Body of Christ. No kingdom divided against itself can stand (Mark 3:24). My fervent prayer is that the Holy Spirit will show us (and me particularly) how to express and implement God's purposes without willfully alienating other believers who may not agree with us.

## UNDERSTANDING THE TEMPLE

*What? know ye not that your body is the temple of the Holy Ghost which is in you, which ye have of God, and ye are not your own? (1Corinthians 6:19)*

In the New Testament, it is clear that our body is the temple where the Holy Spirit dwells. When Jesus spoke of destroying the temple and raising it up again in three days, He was referring to His body (John 2:19-21). The spiritual imagery of the temple is clear. However, the temple I refer to at this time is not our body or the Lord's body, but rather brick and mortar facilities we currently call churches. Specifically, I want you to understand the *concept of the temple* and its purpose in the plan of God.

You can drive through nearly every community in America and find buildings labeled as 'churches'. They run the gamut from store fronts, simple little buildings to elaborate complexes. I recently attended a conference in a church building where there was a quarter mile walk from the auditorium to the youth center – under one roof.

From the early days of my Christian walk, I was greatly inspired by beautiful church buildings. When my wife and I would travel by car, I would regularly stop and attempt to tour churches I spotted from the highway. Atlanta, Georgia was one of our regular destinations, and I probably have toured most of the prominent church buildings that could be seen from I-75 South. In reality, regardless as to how ornate they were, these buildings were not the church, but rather facilities where the church gathered.

As the Lord began to birth this revelation of church structure in my spirit, my view of the physical church building began to evolve. Often I found these building to be beautiful and appealing, but functionally inept.

In the late eighties I served as the Executive Director of a housing program. In this capacity I sat on boards with several presidents and vice–presidents of local banks. The majority of meetings centered around housing for low and moderate income people. At times, the conversation drifted to the bank's policies relating to business lending – specifically to churches.

I was amazed to hear banker after banker describe their resolute conservatism in lending to churches. Their reasoning was even more eye-opening. Here are a few:

- Bankers viewed church income for loan repayment as unstable even in the best of conditions. It was too dependent upon 'voluntary' donations.

- Bankers saw church buildings as 'single use facilities',

meaning that in the unfortunate event of foreclosure there were only a limited number of prospects to sell it to.

- Bankers believed that church buildings, regardless of how elaborate, are usually functionally deficient as an investment. The majority of the building was only used once or twice a week. The financial return on the cost per square foot did not make sense from a business point of view.

- Few churches had 'business plans'. For those that did, they were too often built on 'intangibles' such as faith, belief and hope – nice to have but totally immeasurable by the bank for strategic financial planning.

- The one clear advantage to the bank was the PR (public relations) aspect of a church loan. Within every church is a congregation of potential depositors for the bank. They recognize the economic power of groups, even if the church fails to see it.

- This same PR advantage can backfire in the event of foreclosure. The banker's feared having a congregation 'bad mouthing' them in the community for shutting down their church.

The Lord used this experience to cause me to evaluate my vision of church facilities. At that time I still had the traditional church paradigm, but I clearly began to see the necessity of having a building that made sense from a business perspective.


## THE ENORMOUS COST

I have had the opportunity to sit behind the scenes with 'big name' pastors. An issue I heard too often was the struggle they had meeting church mortgage payments. I personally know two pastors whose mortgage payments are over $25,000 per month each. For one, their mortgage payments exceed forty percent of their overall budget each and every month. Another church I know lost their building to foreclosure. They had built a beautiful facility but it obviously drained all of their resources. A common trait in the church world is that too much money is spent on buildings, compared to the money spent to expand the Kingdom.

Church Real Estate in America is valued in the hundreds of billions of dollars. Debt service and maintenance absorbs up to $11 billion dollars every year from the tithes of the believers. This is startling when you consider the low number of believers who actually tithe. Imagine what $11 billion could do to further the work of ministry. The reality is that buildings will not disappear off of the religious landscape. Financing and constructing 'church' buildings is a multi-billion dollar business.

As church structure changes, a major question that needs to be addressed is 'what will be done with the thousands of church buildings, if many move towards the New Testament model of the church?' You probably expect me to give some glowing theologically deep answer, but the reality is I don't have a clear solution to this question. I will however suggest the following.

When meeting with architects about designing a church building, one of the first questions they ask is 'How do you plan to use the building?' The idea is that usage drives the ultimate design. I believe the temple needs to be understood in its *function* over its design.

What should such a building look like; a few offices for administration, an area for a bookstore, classrooms, private prayer chapels, possibly a dining area and one or two large meeting rooms? Frankly this sounds like some of our existing church buildings. This may lend itself to solving the question of what to do with these buildings. Not only can the above activities be undertaken in the existing facilities, but whole church meetings can held be there as well.

Let's not be overly concerned with its façade as much as what we will do within its walls. My purpose is to outline what I believe I see in the Word of God that took place in the brick and mortar temple. More importantly we need to see how this applies to us today. Remember, I am teaching a concept – not a type of building. Let's turn our attention to what took place in the temple?

## TEACHING

Teaching was a major activity in both the temple and the synagogues. Jesus taught in the synagogues. The apostles often taught in the synagogues.

> *And Jesus returned in the power of the Spirit into Galilee: and there went out a fame of him through all the region round about. And he taught in their synagogues, being glorified of all. And he came to Nazareth, where he had been brought up: and, as his custom was, he went into the synagogue on the sabbath day, and stood up for to read (Luke 4:14-16).*

> *And [Paul] reasoned in the synagogue every sabbath, and persuaded the Jews and the Greeks (Acts 18:4).*

*And [Paul] <u>went into the synagogue, and spake boldly for the space of</u> three months, <u>disputing and persuading</u> the things concerning the kingdom of God (Acts 19:8).*

Paul persuaded and disputed in the synagogue. This implies the synagogue was a place of interaction. In both situations his arguments centered upon 'Jesus Christ and things concerning the kingdom of God'. Teaching appears to be primary activity in both the temple and the synagogue.

The purpose of teaching is not simply to release new information, but it also serves to correct bad information and practices. Often, we need to un-learn some things we have learned

*Go, stand and speak in the temple to the people all the words of this life. And when they heard that, <u>they entered into the temple early in the morning, and taught</u> (Ac 5:20-21a).*

*Then came one and told them, saying, Behold, the men whom ye put in prison are <u>standing in the temple, and teaching the people</u> (Acts 5:25).*

*And <u>daily in the temple, and in every house, they ceased not to teach</u> and preach Jesus Christ (Acts 5:42).*

*And when the seven days were almost ended, the Jews which were of Asia, <u>when they saw him in the temple,</u> stirred up all the people, and laid hands on him, Crying out, Men of Israel, help: <u>This is the man, that teacheth all men</u> every where against the people, and the law, and this place: and further brought Greeks also into the temple, and hath polluted this holy place (Acts 21:27-28).*

## THE PURPOSE OF CHRIST: TEMPLE CONCEPT

Existing church facilities can easily become training centers. They can be a place of continuous teaching. Doctrinal truth must be taught in order to insure continuity and balance in the church. New leaders must be instructed and prepared in an environment conducive for study and learning. It then becomes the place where we discover the *purposes* of Christ.

Teaching will be vital over the next several years. We cannot assume that people will automatically understand New Testament principles, practices and patterns. Therefore teaching, mentoring, exampling and activating believers must be constant and consistent.

Notice most of the scriptures I gave to express activities in the temple. Many of these passages express that Jesus and the Apostles 'taught' in the temple. We know whatever they taught was good, but it is more important to remember that whatever the subject matter— they taught it. This is very important to understand.

Some have argued that teaching New Testament practice is solely the work of the Holy Spirit. They further state that all we need to do is preach Jesus – His death, burial and resurrection – and everything else will fall into place. Others assert that the 'organic nature' of the New Testament church creates a Holy Spirit led atmosphere that eliminates the need for formalized teaching. Scripture contradicts this thinking and I believe these arguments are naive.

The doctrines of Jesus Christ and His Kingdom were fresh revelation in the first century. The Holy Spirit had been poured out, but apparently He worked in concert with the apostle's teachings (Acts 2:42; Titus 2:1). Jesus taught the Kingdom. He mentored twelve men. Paul and the other apostles taught in the temples. Priscilla and Acquila taught Apollos. Paul mentored and taught Timothy, Titus, Silas and Silvaneus. Teaching is an important factor that must not be overlooked. This is not limited to teaching the doctrines of Christ, but also the practices of His Church (1Corinthians 11:2; 1Timothy 3:15; Hebrews 10:25).

History is replete with reformers who established teaching centers to promulgate the truths they espoused. We credit Martin Luther with the birth of the Protestant reformation. But we must remember that soon after leaving the Roman Catholic Church he set up schools to train former priests in his doctrine and practices.

Later, John Wesley received a revelation of holiness. He too established schools to teach his revelation. The list goes on with John Calvin, William Seymour, Charles Mason, Oral Roberts, Kenneth Hagin, Bill Hamon, Peter Wagner and so on. All of these men preached the Gospel of Jesus Christ, and found it necessary to establish training centers to build strong foundations pertaining to both doctrine and practices.

The purpose of teaching is not simply to release new information, but it also serves to correct bad information and practices. Often, we need to un-learn some things we have learned (Jeremiah 1:10).

This time of transition in the church is no different. As the church moves toward a more organic structure, there must be solid regional training centers that serve to lay clear apostolic foundations. This will be accented with apostolic teams who serve in regions in order to help plant New Testament Churches and train leadership.

The Holy Spirit is important to the success of any reformation. He confirms in the spirit that earthly practices are the will of the

Father. (John 14:26; 16:13-15). In every matter we work in sync with the Holy Spirit (Acts 15:28). The Bride (the earthly Body of Christ) must work in close conjunction with the Holy Spirit (Revelation 22:17).


## PRAYER

Prayer, both personal and corporate was commonly held in the temple.

> *Now Peter and John went up together <u>into the temple at the hour of prayer</u>, being the ninth hour (Acts 3:1)*

> *And it came to pass, that, when I was come again to Jerusalem, <u>even while I prayed in the temple</u>, I was in a trance (Acts 22:17)*

The 21st century *temple* should be a place for prayer. Corporate times of prayer should be established. Church facilities should always have rooms available for believers to get alone and commune with God.

The first century temple had a lot of activity surrounding it. After Pentecost, the believers seemed to hang around the temple every day (Acts 2:46). Beggars like the lame man in Acts 3 found the outer courts of the temple a great place to beg. Obviously the crowds made it lucrative. Remember, Jesus dealt with money changers in the temple (John 2:14-15).

When Jesus ran the money changers out of the temple, he was not making an indictment against selling goods. He was dealing with the unfair advantage those that bought and sold were taking over those who needed items for sacrifice.

We see then that the first century temple was also a business hub. Therefore we can conclude that the 21st century temple can be a place to conduct business. Bookstores and administrative offices are proper activities to have in our church facilities.

What have we gleaned from all this? In the first century the synagogue and temple was a place where doctrinal issues were argued. It was a place where teaching took place regularly, and it was a gathering place for prayer. The 21st century temple can serve as a place for settling matters that affect the church. I cannot definitively state that the dispute over circumcising the Gentiles in Acts 15 was held in the temple, but I can say that this type of discussion could easily take place in a temple or synagogue setting.

## RESTORING PATTERNS

The work of ministry is being preceded by a return to New Testament patterns and practices. As stated earlier, this is not a return to togas and sandals, but a return to a structure that supported growth of the Kingdom in the earth.

This will require a return to simple gatherings in homes as the primary church. There will be a return to oversight by a plurality of elders and development of the saints by five–fold ministry gifts. Multitudes of believers will effectively reach their communities with the Gospel of the Kingdom, because the concept of laity was not found in the New Testament era.

I believe within the next ten years, thousands of existing churches will change the way they operate, and many new churches built on New Testament patterns will emerge. Are you ready?

# Biblical Structure and Order 6

In the last chapter I established that the church is a three–fold entity consisting of (1) the house gatherings, (2) the whole church and (3) the temple. All three components are necessary to have a church established in New Testament patterns. Our Sunday morning only worship that is most common today is an incomplete model reflecting only the whole church with some classes. The gathering in the house has been largely neglected.

## THE CELL CHURCH

You may be in a church that has small groups that meet regularly. These small groups are usually called cells. I thank God for *cell churches*, and *churches with cell groups* (there is a difference). They both are a step in the right direction. *Cell churches* provide a structure similar to the New Testament model. There is however a significant difference.

Generally speaking, even when you consider all of the variations of cell groups, they still exist as an offshoot of the larger corporate church. With the cell church structure, the cells exist at the behest of the larger corporate church. If the leadership of the larger corporate church determines that the cell program should end – then they cease. The purpose for cell groups varies depending on the church. Some use them for evangelism and church growth, while others use them for specialty groups such as divorce, addiction support groups or pastoral care.

Individual participation is often regulated in the cells. Often it is controlled participation. Specific roles are established to give the larger corporate church a means to monitor what takes place in the small group meeting. As such, cells are often a duplication of the institutional church structure. Even if there are similar activities taking place in the cell group as in the house churches, the key thing to understand is that the larger corporate church is considered '*the church*' and cells are generally an activity, a program, a ministry or mission within it.

In the New Testament, the small gatherings of believers in houses are the church. They are independent as well as inter-dependent. Rather than being an offshoot of the larger corporate church, the larger church exists because of them. Without the house churches, there is little need for the larger church. The larger church has been previously defined as the whole church.

The larger church or whole church is the spiritual support network for the house churches. The larger church or whole church is not it's building, but the coming together of several house churches in a city or region. (Acts 15:22; Romans 16:23; 1Corinthians 14:23).

## GOD'S VIEW OF STRUCTURE

The way a thing is structured is important to God. Structure brings definition and validates divine intent. No where in scripture did God allow things to be formed in a haphazard way. He was always explicit in structure and order. Our failure to obey His instructions is done at our own peril.

We have previously stated that church structure is not a doctrine. Nevertheless, you can also see examples of structures in scripture that were built from clear directions from God. In every situation, the structure served to reveal and perpetuate the purposes of God in the earth. The structure itself was not to be worshipped (Exodus 20:3-4; Leviticus 26:1). This applies to the church today. Its structure, as important as it is, is not to be worshipped.

The structure is the catalyst by which the purposes of God can be fully revealed and perpetuated in the earth. His will is that the saints do the work of ministry (Ephesians 4:11-12). The structure of the New Testament church must be conducive to that end.

Structure defines order. It clarifies the function of each part. This is critical as we will see later. The modern day church has unknowingly distorted biblical order to match its incomplete structure. Five-fold ministry gifts are adjusted to fit the institutionally structured church. Elders and deacons are tossed around in various roles solely dependent on the church system. In every case biblical roles have been made to fit the church system, rather than the church system adjusting to the biblical roles.

## UNDERSTANDING STRUCTURE

Before we go further, it is necessary to have a working definition of *church structure.* Please read the following carefully:

THE CHURCH IS A HUMAN STRUCTURE, BUILT BY DIVINE PATTERN, FOR ETERNAL PURPOSES.

Jesus is building His Church. It is not being constructed in heaven. The Church is being constructed on the earth. The church is a building not made with hands (Acts 7:48; Hebrews 9:11). The church is being built with people, like you and me who have been washed in His blood and filled with His Spirit (Ephesians 2:19-22; 1Peter 2:5). To first say that the church is a *'human structure'* is to express that the church is comprised of people, not brick and mortar. It is also to say that the church is built with components we understand, but organized and assembled by divine instructions. That leads us to the next part.

*For the body is not one member, but many. If the foot shall say, Because I am not the hand, I am not of the body; is it therefore not of the body? And if the ear shall say, Because I am not the eye, I am not of the body; is it therefore not of the body? If the whole body were an eye, where were the hearing? If the whole were hearing, where were the smelling? But now hath God set the members every one of them in the body, as it hath pleased him. And if they were all one member, where were the body? But now are they many members, yet but one body. And the eye cannot say unto the hand, I have no need of thee: nor again the head to the feet, I have no need of you. Nay, much more those members of the body, which seem to be more feeble, are necessary: And those members of the body, which we think to be less honourable, upon these we bestow more abundant honour; and our uncomely parts have more abundant comeliness. (1Corinthians 12:14-23)*

David wrote that we are fearfully and wonderfully made (Psalms 139:14). God designed each part of us to function in its designated place. This is divine pattern.

God personally set each member in the body as it pleased Him. The members did not place themselves into position. Paul made it clear that each part is valuable to the body. In order for its value to be recognized, it must be in the right place.

When Ezekiel prophesied to the dry bones in the valley, they eventually became a great army. But structurally, they first had to come together – not just any way – but each bone had to connect properly with the other bones. The King James Version specifically said that each bone came to *his bone* (Ezekiel 37:7). In other words, each bone recognized another bone necessary for it to fulfill its purpose.

No part of the body can fully function without the other parts, but this is exactly what the modern day church has done. We have tried to *'go it alone'* either in personal ministry or denominational separatism. Everyone acts as though they have no need for the rest of the body. The enemy is able to destroy and weaken these disconnected parts with secularism, humanism and false doctrines.

Another important factor that is revealed in Paul's letter to the Corinthians is *capacity.* "If the foot shall say, Because I am not the hand, I am not of the body; is it therefore not of the body? And if the ear shall say, Because I am not the eye, I am not of the body; is it therefore not of the body?"

The foot is designed by God to help bear the weight of the body, but the ear is not. The ear is designed by God to receive external sound and forward it to the brain for deciphering. The hands can grasp and take hold of things, but the eyes can only recognize them with the help of the brain. In other words, the ear does not have the God given *capacity* to do what the foot does. If it tried, it would be a dismal failure. The eyes cannot do what the hand does. If the eye physically tried to grasp something, it would destroy itself.

No part of the body was ever given the capacity to function outside of their set place. Today, we have so many dysfunctional and misplaced 'part' ministries that the Body of Christ is deformed and irrelevant to the world. The reason is that too many parts are attempting to do ministry they are not divinely equipped to do.

The church is a human structure, built by divine pattern, but ultimately it exists for God's eternal purpose.

*To the intent that now unto the principalities and powers in heavenly places might be known by the church the manifold wisdom of God, According to the eternal purpose which he purposed in Christ Jesus our Lord (Ephesians 3:10-11)*

It is God's ultimate purpose that the church demonstrates His wisdom to principalities and powers in the earth. This was His purpose from the foundation of the world.

The Church was never intended to be a spiritual babysitting service for beleaguered Christians waiting for their trip out of the earth through the rapture. The Church is to be a strong army that systematically defeats the forces of darkness through Jesus Christ. The gates of hell can't prevail against it (Matthew 16:18). The enemies of God will be defeated by it (1Corinthians 15:24-26). Through the Church, the Kingdom of God will be proclaimed and demonstrated in the earth (Matthew 24:14).

## OLD TESTAMENT EXAMPLES OF STRUCTURE

The bible is very consistent in dealing with God's view of structure. As we examine various structures in the Old Testament, God may reveal to you the value of embracing the New Testament structure of the church.

### Noah's Ark

The ark was a human structure, built by divine pattern for eternal purposes.

> The earth also was corrupt before God, and the earth was filled with violence. And God looked upon the earth, and, behold, it was corrupt; for all flesh had corrupted his way upon the earth. And God said unto Noah, The end of all flesh is come before me; for the earth is filled with violence through them; and, behold, I will destroy them with the earth. Make thee an ark of gopher wood; rooms shalt thou make in the ark, and shalt pitch it within and without with pitch. And this is the fashion which thou shalt make it of: The length of the ark shall be three hundred cubits, the breadth of it fifty cubits, and the height of it thirty cubits. A window shalt thou make to the ark, and in a cubit shalt thou finish it above; and the door of the ark shalt thou set in the side thereof; with lower, second, and third stories shalt thou make it. And, behold, I, even I, do bring a flood of waters upon the earth, to destroy all flesh, wherein is the breath of life, from under heaven; and every thing that is in the earth shall die

*(Genesis 6:11-17).*

God was very specific in instructing Noah how to build the ark. Keep in mind that Noah had never seen an ark; he did not know how it would work, nor did he understand the concept of rain or flood (Genesis 2:5). What he did understand was the components of the ark and he understood God's instructions in bringing them together.

Noah knew what gopher wood was, but he did not know that wood would one day come to symbolize humanity. Noah knew what pitch was, but he did not understand that the Hebrew word *kaphar* that pitch was translated from figuratively reflects the atonement. Noah obediently constructed a window in the ark that in the Hebrew language literally means light. We know today that the entrance of God's word gives light or revelation (Psalms 119:130). Noah also made a door, not knowing that thousands of years later that Jesus would declare Himself the only door to the Father (John 10:7-9).

This book cannot cover all the revelation that pours out of the story of Noah, but suffice it to say that the purposes of God were fulfilled in his day. The flood came and the ark provided the safety necessary for Noah and his family. Imagine what would have happened had Noah decided to build the ark after his own design? Likewise, consider the condition of the church. Is it God's design or is it a reflection of something built in man's design?

The Tabernacle In The Wilderness

The Tabernacle was a human structure, built by divine pattern for eternal purposes.

> *And thou shalt rear up the tabernacle according to the fashion thereof which was shewed thee in the mount (Exodus 26:30)*

*Our fathers had the tabernacle of witness in the wilderness, as he had appointed, speaking unto Moses, that he should make it according to the fashion that he had seen (Acts 7:44)*

*...as Moses was admonished of God when he was about to make the tabernacle: for, See, saith he, that thou make all things according to the pattern shewed to thee in the mount (Hebrews 8:5)*

The most notable thing we see in the building of the Tabernacle was that Moses received a clear revelation of its pattern and structure (Exodus Chapters 26-27). As you study the story in depth, you will also find that Moses was given clear instructions as to who was to do what in the building and care of the Tabernacle. Notice how specific God was:

We have innocently operated in our most common church system for 1,700 years. This is all we have ever known. Therefore, how we do church today is primary out of ignorance.

*This shall be the service of the sons of Kohath in the tabernacle of the congregation, about the most holy things (Numbers 4:4)*

*This is the service of the families of the Gershonites, to serve, and for burdens: And they shall bear the curtains of the tabernacle, and the tabernacle of the congregation, his covering, and the covering of the badgers' skins that is above upon it, and the hanging for the door of the tabernacle of the congregation (Numbers 4:24-25),*

*This is the service of the families of the sons of Merari, according to all their service, in the tabernacle of the congregation, under the hand of*

*Ithamar the son of Aaron the priest (Numbers 4:33)*

These passages alert us to two things. First, God is specific about the design of His work in the earth and, second, He is specific about who does His work. If we can ever get a revelation of this truth much of the chaos in the church would disappear.

The Tabernacle was built in the wilderness after the Israelites had been freed from four hundred years of bondage. God established the Tabernacle after they were physically free. It took ten plagues to free them from Egypt, but forty years to free the Egyptian slave mentality from them.

The structure of the New Testament church has not been as ignored as it has been unknown. We have innocently operated in our most common church system for 1,700 years. This is all we have ever known. Therefore, how we do church today is primarily out of ignorance. God is presently allowing the Holy Spirit to stir in the hearts of men and women the desire for things greater than what is provided in the current church structure.

Jesus Christ is still building His Church. Throughout the earth apostles and prophets have been to the mount of revelation and are seeing a divine pattern from the Throne of God for His Church that must be constructed in the earth.

## The Breach

I will conclude this chapter with the story of David attempting to move the Ark of the Covenant to Zion. I pray this familiar story will help you to see where the church is today, as well as reinforce how important structure and order is to God.

*Again, David gathered together all the chosen men of Israel, thirty thousand. And David arose, and went with all the people that were with him from Baale of Judah, to bring up from thence the ark of God, whose name is called by the name of the LORD of hosts that dwelleth between the cherubims. And they set the ark of God upon a new cart, and brought it out of the house of Abinadab that was in Gibeah: and Uzzah and Ahio, the sons of Abinadab, drave the new cart. And they brought it out of the house of Abinadab which was at Gibeah, accompanying the ark of God: and Ahio went before the ark. And David and all the house of Israel played before the LORD on all manner of instruments made of fir wood, even on harps, and on psalteries, and on timbrels, and on cornets, and on cymbals. ¶ And when they came to Nachon's threshingfloor, Uzzah put forth his hand to the ark of God, and took hold of it; for the oxen shook it. And the anger of the LORD was kindled against Uzzah; and God smote him there for his error; and there he died by the ark of God. And David was displeased, because the LORD had made a breach upon Uzzah: and he called the name of the place Perezuzzah to this day. And David was afraid of the LORD that day, and said, How shall the ark of the LORD come to me? So David would not remove the ark of the LORD unto him into the city of David: but David carried it aside into the house of Obededom the Gittite. And the ark of the LORD continued in the house of Obededom the Gittite three months: and the LORD blessed Obededom, and all his household (2Samuel 6:1-11)*

David's desire to bring the Ark of the Covenant to his city was admirable. The Ark represented the presence of God. Desiring  God's presence seemed to be the right thing to do.

To the average by-stander David did all the right things. He gathered thirty thousand of the best men. He then commissioned a new cart to carry the Ark, and the praise began. They danced, they sang, they rejoiced because the Ark (the presence of the Lord) was on its way to the City of David.

In route, they passed through Nachon's threshing floor. In the Chaldean version of this story, they came near to the place that was prepared for the Ark. It was in this place that the oxen stumbled, and fearing that the Ark would fall off the cart, Uzzah instinctively reached out to steady it on the cart, and within seconds he was dead.

The music stopped. The dancing stopped. The singing stopped. Everything came to a sudden standstill. What happened? Why was this man killed trying to do the right thing? The bible says that David was displeased. He could not understand why God would interrupt the seemingly glorious activities.

Let's stop here and see how this applies to the church today.

I am convinced that most Christians desire to please the Lord. Their praise, their worship, their dance and their songs are all to give glory to Him. However, like David, we get excited in doing things *for* God, and neglect to discover what is *of* God. Remember the new cart they used to carry the Ark? It was a manmade vehicle that I am sure was made especially for this task. But human intentions are no substitute for obedience (1Samuel 15:22).

Like the cart, the modern day church has become a man-made vehicle especially designed to carry the things of God. We attempt to transport the presence of God using methodologies that are completely unsupported by scripture. Like David, we surround ourselves with the noble men, but fail to find out if they are the chosen men of God. Ministry is done by professionals rather than the faithful.

Our activities, as noble as they may be, are often man-made events and programs that only express our concept of God. This began in the third century when Constantine opened the door to build ornate cathedrals similar to pagan temples for the purpose of worshiping God. When the cathedrals grew, history shows that the church stopped growing. Instead of the organic multiplying that took place from their house to house fellowship, the believers huddled in these cathedrals that were void of spiritual life. In other words, they touched the presence of God in the wrong place and died.

*So David would not remove the ark of the LORD unto him into the city of David: but David carried it aside into the house of Obededom the Gittite. And the ark of the LORD continued in the house of Obededom the Gittite three months: and the LORD blessed Obededom, and all his household (2Samuel 6:10-11)*

David wisely brought all the religious festivities to a halt. The Ark was entrusted to one of his bodyguards, Obededom. For three months the Ark remained there, and Obededom and his house was tremendously blessed. Please note two things.

First, Obededom's house was blessed. Within three months there was such a visible blessing to this man's house that it garnered the attention of David. Second, the fact that Obededom's house was blessed brought proof that Uzzah's death stemmed from the way the Ark was handled. There is no history of anyone in Obededom's house dying as a result of the Ark being there.

When David learned how blessed Obededom was, he made another attempt to transport the Ark. This time he was wiser, and his instructions are vital for us today.

*And David called for Zadok and Abiathar the priests, and for the*

*Levites, for Uriel, Asaiah, and Joel, Shemaiah, and Eliel, and Amminadab, And said unto them, Ye are the chief of the fathers of the Levites: sanctify yourselves, both ye and your brethren, that ye may bring up the ark of the LORD God of Israel unto the place that I have prepared for it. <u>For because ye did it not at the first, the LORD our God made a breach upon us, for that we sought him not after the due order.</u> So the priests and the Levites sanctified themselves to bring up the ark of the LORD God of Israel. And the children of the Levites bare the ark of God upon their shoulders with the staves thereon, as Moses commanded according to the word of the LORD (1Chronicles 15:11-15).*

David realized that transporting the Ark on a cart was error. All of the praise, the worship, the music, the dancing and singing could not override their error. He understood that Uzzah died because they failed to seek the Lord's order. Too often we believe our spiritual actions validate what we do for God.

God never intended for the Ark to be transported on a cart, regardless as to how new it was. The Ark was always to be transported on the shoulders of the priests. This is good news for us today. God is not going to change His structure or order to appease human religious fervor. His presence must always be carried on the shoulders of the priest (Numbers 4:15).

One of the clear values of the New Testament church is to embrace the priesthood of every believer. Every believer is a priest to the Lord (1Peter 2:9; Revelation 1:6). Each of us are entrusted with carrying the presence of the Lord wherever we go. And like Obededom, the presence of the Lord has been entrusted to our homes and others will see we are a blessed people.

God never intended for His Church to be hemmed up in

buildings. He did not institute a clergy and lay class. Yet, the church has continued to carry the presence of the Lord on man-made carts. But now, the Lord is revealing to apostles and prophets in the earth His 'due order'. No longer can we be satisfied transporting the Lord's presence in structures that don't bring Him glory. It is time to stop doing church as usual.

# No Longer Church Government As Usual

**7**

All structures, natural or manmade, have order. Order is maintained by a definable system of government. Order spells out responsibility and authority of those entrusted to run the government. Government therefore is a system of rule. It can be explicit or implicit. Its rules can be accepted as the norm or they can be forced upon someone.

For example, when designing a building, there are architectural rules that govern the building process. These rules spell out in explicit detail the load bearing capacity of the foundation, certain walls and entrances. There are rules governing how the electrical and plumbing systems are to work. Failure to obey those rules can result in catastrophe.

Plant life has organic rules of nature that govern the health of fruit, vegetables and flowers. Violation of the organic rules (i.e. deprivation of sun, water, etc.) will result in weak or worthless plants. Whether you realize it or not, your body has divine laws that govern your health. Violation of these laws (smoking, lack of rest, overeating, etc.) can result in sickness or premature death.

Let's consider the church. The church is a living organism. All organisms have some level of organization. When something is organized, it implies there are systems and rules that govern it.

How do you govern an entity that is both visible and invisible? It is an invisible Holy Habitation built from visible 'lively stones'. It is perceived as an invisible 'body' with visible 'members in particular'. The health of the New Testament church is linked to understanding its government. If the government is weak, the long term viability and stability of the church will be jeopardized. If the government is too rigid or controlling, the church will be cold and stagnant. Without an understanding of how New Testament church government functions, there will be confusion at best, and anarchy at worst. If the people governed do not know or have confidence in their leaders, fear and mistrust will reign.

The church (both visible and invisible) is the representative of God's Kingdom in the earth. Therefore, it must reflect the government of the Kingdom. Although we give mental and verbal assent to this fact, by in large, we still function governmentally under a non-biblical institutional model. We have operated this way so long that when we are given a glimpse of the biblical model, the biblical model is what seems to be in error.

In his book, THE CHURCH IN THE NEW TESTAMENT, Dr. Kevin J. Connor devoted an entire chapter challenging the current traditional church system. He aptly named the chapter, *Challenge To Change The Traditional System.* He listed five areas that would strike any believer who would give an 'unbiased reading' of the Book of Acts and the church Epistles. In clear detail he dealt with (1) t*he absence of the Monarchal or One-Man Pastoral System;* (2) *the plurality of Eldership in the Church;* (3) *the local government of the Church;* (4) *the five-fold ascension gift ministries;* and (5) the *absence of Titular Authority.*[3]

Like most of those reading this book, I grew up in a traditional church setting. I was saved in the traditional church. Thousands are still being saved in the traditional church. I am not at war with the church structure as we have known it. Frankly, I don't believe God is angry with anyone who worships in traditional church settings. I did not know of any other way to worship, nor did I know to look for or expect anything different.

I completely understand and empathize with those who are reluctant to embrace the structural changes I teach in this book. But the fact remains, when you know different – you do different. We should all be on a constant quest to line up with the Word of God in principle, practice and value. That is why I urge you to examine what you read in this book by the Word of God.

## SEEING THE END OF THE STORY

It is God's divine intent to establish the fullness of His Kingdom in the earth. From the beginning when man was instructed to be fruitful, to multiply, to replenish and subdue the earth, God established a plan to redeem all that was lost by sin in the Garden (Genesis 1:28). He chose to recapture the earth and defeat satan through an army of obedient men and women.

Adam's sin in the Garden was an act of treason. His act of disobedience gave satan access to the earth. The devil took claim to all that belonged to God (Luke 4:5-7). But God's plan was not deterred. He will still recapture all that was stolen from Him through an army of obedient men and women – His Church.

Jesus taught us to pray 'thy kingdom come' (Matthew 6:10). He taught there would be kingdom warfare (Matthew 24:7). But scripture also declares that in the end, Jesus will triumphantly submit the Kingdom to God (1Corinthians 15:24). Then will come the eternal announcement that the kingdoms of this world have become the Kingdom of our God and His Christ (Revelations 11:15).

We are at war. The Kingdom of God is waging battle with the kingdoms of darkness. The outcome is sure. The Kingdom of God will prevail (Isaiah 60:12; Daniel 2:44; 7:14, 27; Luke 1:33; 1Corinthians 15:24). This war is not being fought without strategy. Each of us who have submitted our lives to Jesus Christ are called into divine service. We each play a significant part in the ultimate defeat of satan and his kingdom. The ultimate idea or belief we carry within us is that God's rule will encompass the universe (1Corinthians 15:28). This is the underlying reason we need to understand God's government in His church.

## DEFINING CHURCH GOVERNMENT

*Government is a system of rule and oversight of people necessary to insure the perpetuity of an ideology or set of beliefs.* Government affects how smoothly an entity operates. It details roles and responsibilities. It would be too cumbersome to try and describe in detail every form of church government in existence (i.e. Congregational, Presbytery, Episcopal).

Instead, I will outline the government necessary to oversee the New Testament church advocated in this book.

## ALL GOVERNMENTS ARE ROOTED IN IDEOLOGY

Government is first driven by an ideology. You have probably heard terms such as democratic government, socialist government or communist government. Each of these governments is defined by an ideology or set of beliefs that describe how they believe things should be – democratic, socialist and communist. Likewise you are familiar with terms like Baptist church, Methodist church, Pentecostal church, etc. Each church is defined by an ideology or set of beliefs – Baptist, Methodist, Pentecostal, etc.

Whether the idea begins with one person or a group of people, once it is fully embraced, it becomes the driving force to establish an order or system of rule that insures the perpetuity of that ideology or belief. This is government. An order or system of rule employed to oversee and protect the perpetuity of the idea.

Government is exercised within defined territories. The proponents of certain ideologies often desire to export their beliefs to other territories. Some use diplomacy to plant their ideas into the soil of the hearts of men and women in foreign lands. Others try to forcefully impose their government over other territories. This is an important distinction. Diplomacy often wins the hearts of people. They embrace the ideas and beliefs being presented to them and willfully submit to the government necessary to oversee and protect the ideas and beliefs. On the other hand, if a government is forcefully imposed upon a person, it does not insure that the ideas and beliefs that drive that government are embraced or accepted.

## THE NATURE OF CHURCH GOVERNMENT

The nature of New Testament church government is rooted in *influence, respect* and *mutual submission*. It is not hierarchal or top down ruled.


## NO HIERARCHY

The New Testament is completely void of the hierarchy which is prevalent in the institutional church mindset. The bible clearly emphasizes *function* over *title*. The '*top-down*' leadership model found in most churches is not biblical (Matthew 20:25-28; Mark 10:42-45; Luke 22:25-27; 1Peter 5:3). It is borrowed from the Constantinian model imposed upon the church around the third century. Top-down leadership subtly or overtly demands submission from those considered beneath the leader.

Because of this 'hierarchal' thinking, it is difficult for some to envision leadership who serve in an atmosphere of *influence by example, respect based on equality in Christ, and mutual submission emanating from understanding each others function*. As long as hierarchy is prevalent in one's thinking, then leadership function will take a back seat to leadership status.

Paul's letters to various churches reflect the heart of a father bringing direction, correction and protection to his children. As much as these believers loved the Lord, from time to time their actions required the loving but firm hand of an apostolic father to guide them. His letters reveal the influence he had in their lives, the shared respect between him and the church, and the mutual submission they gave to each other.

An example of this is found when Paul sternly addressed the Corinthian believers for tolerating the sin of a young man who committed adultery with his father's wife. He gave them explicit instructions as to how this matter should be dealt with (1Corinthians 5:1-6).

Apparently, they took Paul's instructions to heart and nearly went overboard in disciplining the young man. Paul had to write them again and instruct them to also be willing to forgive and restore the young man (2Corinthians 2:5-8).

> In the exercise of church government, no man has a right to claim dominion over your faith

In this matter, Paul demonstrated the nature of church government. He had influence on the Corinthian believers. Yet, he made it clear that he did not have dominion over their faith, revealing his respect for them (2Corinthians 1:24), He also asserted that he had earthly authority to bring correction and test their obedience (1Corinthians 9:2; 2Corinthians 2:9).

In the exercise of church government, no man has a right to claim dominion over your faith. Yet, in the Lord's design for His church, there are those who are given to govern in the earth to insure that Kingdom values, principles and practices are exercised. It is up to the believers to decide their level of obedience. The authority given to earthly governors cannot cross over the line into the realm of control.

## PEOPLE AND LEADERSHIP

Governments cover a defined territory. It impacts the people of that territory. It is actuated by defined leadership. You cannot impose the laws of the United States on the people of India. We would not tolerate the Prime Minister of Great Britain attempting to run our country. A citizen of Newark, New Jersey would not be allowed to vote in a local election in Battle Creek, Michigan. We inherently understand the boundaries of political governments, but often are confused with the boundaries in the church.

Similar to the dichotomy of the church being visible and invisible, the church is also both universal and local. There is the global Body of Christ and there is the local expression of the Body of Christ. In the local arena, there is the 'city church' which is composed of local assemblies, including 'house churches'. Watchman Nee, in 1939 published a work entitled *Concerning Our Missions.* In it he described the difference between the universal Church and local church as follows:

> We have clearly two different aspects of the Church before us – the Church and the churches. The Church is invisible; the churches are visible. The Church has no organization; the churches are organized. The Church is spiritual; the churches are spiritual and yet physical. The Church is purely an organism; the churches are an organism, yet at the same time they are organized, which is seen by the fact that elders and deacons hold office there.[4]

It is in the local expression of the churches that human government becomes necessary. Note that Watchman Nee specifically mentions elders and deacons in connection with the local churches. That is because elders bear the weight of overseeing the local churches, and deacons serve with them. Some have erroneously thought that apostles and the other five fold ministry gifts oversee the local church. They have their place in the churches as we will discuss later, but the oversight of the churches is the primary responsibility of local elders.

In the Word of God, the universal Church has no boundaries, but the local churches are always referred to by locality and house churches are referred to by the homeowner.

*And Saul was consenting unto his death. And at that time there was a great persecution against the church which was at Jerusalem; and they were all scattered abroad throughout the regions of Judaea and Samaria, except the apostles. (Acts 8:1)*

There was persecution against the local church identified as *the church which was at Jerusalem.* As a result, the people were scattered throughout the regions around Jerusalem.

*Then had the churches rest throughout all Judaea and Galilee and Samaria, and were edified; and walking in the fear of the Lord, and in the comfort of the Holy Ghost, were multiplied. (Acts 9:31)*

Note that the churches (plural) had rest in the regions. In the regions of Judaea, Galilee and Samaria there were several cities where the believers settled and started new churches. It is the same pattern seen throughout scripture. The local church is known by the city.

*Now there were in the church that was at Antioch ... (Acts 13:1)*

*And when he had landed at Caesarea, and gone up, and saluted the church... (Acts 18:22)*

*I commend unto you Phebe our sister, which is a servant of the church which is at Cenchrea: (Romans 16:1)*

*Unto the church of God which is at Corinth... (1Corinthians 1:2)*

*Paul, and Silvanus, and Timotheus, unto the church of the Thessalonians... (2Thessalonians 1:1)*

When John penned the Book of Revelation, he began by writing seven churches in Asia, each identified by a city - Ephesus, Smyrna, Pergamos, Thyatira, Sardis, Philadelphia, and Laodicea (Revelation 1:11).

Within each locality, there were apparently specific meeting places. These were the house churches. House churches were identified by the homeowner or homeowners. References were made to the church in the houses of Aquila and Priscilla (Romans 16:3-5; 1Corinthians 16:19), Nymphas (Colossians 4:15), Philemon (Philemon 1:1-2), Jason (Acts 17:5), Chloe (1Corinthians 1:11), Lydia (Acts 16:40) and Mary (Acts 12:12). Although these individuals were mentioned by name, it by no means implies that they were the only house churches in a particular locality.

On the day of Pentecost, three thousand became believers (Acts 2:41). Shortly thereafter, another five thousand became believers (Acts 4:4). With no explanation, scripture simply states that the Lord added to the church as a result of this massive influx of people who met from house to house (Acts 2:46-47). It is specifically interesting to note that the apostles did not call for a massive building project to erect synagogues, temples or any other physical structures to accommodate these believers. They simply met from house to house from the beginning of the church and continued that pattern until the third century.

Let's review the structure of the New Testament church again. This structure must be understood in order to appreciate its government.

First, there is the universal Church – the Body of Christ worldwide. Secondly, there is the local church identified by the name of the city. There could be the church in Albion, Battle Creek, New York, London or any other city you choose to name. Within each city you will find many house churches. House churches are identified by the name of the homeowner. It could be the church in the house of Tim and Carolyn, or Ed and Margaret, or Victor and Carol or literally thousands of other house churches. The house church is the most basic and foundational level of the church.

To be specific, there is the Body of Christ worldwide. Then there are defined regions which can be as expansive as the entire country, a state but most likely a territory similar to a county. Understanding this structure, drawn from the writings of the New Testament, will make it easier for you to embrace the government of the Church.

## GOVERNING THE NEW TESTAMENT CHURCH STRUCTURE

Government is the system of rule and oversight of people necessary to insure the perpetuity of an idea.

Governance begins with the individual. Self governance is the highest level of governing possible. It is the free will choice of an individual to embrace, support and perpetuate an idea through word and action. Self governance is the individual choice to live holy without the need of external directives. It is the choice to do what is right, instead of being constrained to do what is right.

Self governing is *internal* in nature. It is supported by peers. This is commonly known as accountability. It is when the individual connects with a group of like minded individuals. Collectively, the group embraces the idea, and through word and action encourages everyone among them to do the same. This is an important level of governance. At this level, there may be those who don't fully understand the idea or belief and need others to encourage and strengthen them.

There is also *external* governing. This is necessary for those who don't embrace the idea. Some go as far as trying to undermine, weaken, dismantle or destroy it. It then becomes the responsibility of those who are entrusted to protect against any individuals, groups or things that can harm the idea or the people following it. This is external government.

A *permissional society* does not mean that everyone does what they want when they want to. Therefore *permissional* is not to be confused with *permissive*. By no means is a permissional society a religious free-for-all

The 'idea' I keep referencing is in the heart of God. It is His truth alone. (Psalms 33:11; Proverbs 19:21; Isaiah 46:9-10).

It is His idea to establish His Kingdom in the earth (Daniel 2:44; 7:27; Luke 1:32-33; 1Corinthians 15:24). It was His idea to send His Son into the earth to build a church of blood-washed sons and daughters (Matthew 16:18; John 1:12; 1Corinthians 6:20). It is His idea to entrust His church to spread His Kingdom rule throughout the land (Genesis 1:28; Ephesians 3:10). God alone has determined the times, seasons, and methodologies by which His 'idea' will be accomplished (Acts 1:7; Ephesians 3:3-6). Self governance, accountability and protective governance all center around God's idea.

## SELF GOVERNANCE AND ACCOUNTABILITY IN THE CHURCH

The less internal government you have, the more external government you need. A person in prison requires more external government because they lack the internal government necessary to keep them from committing crimes. In the church of the Lord Jesus Christ, if you are unable to hear and follow the Holy Spirit in the choices you make, it may require external direction until you are able to do so. This principle is clearly laid out in scripture.

> And thou shalt teach them ordinances and laws, and shalt shew them the way wherein they must walk, and the work that they must do. (Exodus 18:20)

> Now I say, That the heir, as long as he is a child, differeth nothing from a servant, though he be lord of all; But is under tutors and governors until the time appointed of the father. (Galatians 4:1-2)

## A PERMISSIONAL SOCIETY

The government of the New Testament church begins with self governance. It is the free will choice to embrace the idea in word and action. It is when we 'confess with our mouth and believe in our hearts' that Jesus is Lord (Romans 10:9-10). Confession is done externally whereas belief is internal. The external confession and the internal belief must be in sync (Psalms 19:14; Mark 11:23). Too often people have lived on lip service, having no intention of obeying the Word of God (Isaiah 29:13; Matthew 15:8). As confession and belief synchronize, a believer literally becomes more submitted to the Lord Jesus Christ in all they do.

Every citizen of the Kingdom of God is a king and priest with both ministry and redemptive authority. We exercise our ministry and kingdom authority in the earth – not heaven (Romans 5:17; 2Corinthians 5:18; Revelation 5:10).

If you understand that you are a king, you also need to understand how to function as a king. A king does not need the permission of another king to exercise his rule and authority. He is permitted by nature of his office to make whatever decisions he deems necessary for the benefit of his kingdom. Thus, we discover the *permissional* aspect of church government. In essence, the church as a whole is a *permissional society*. You are permitted, by nature of your kingly authority, to pursue your assignment in the earth.

The term *permissional* implies the on-going granting of permission by a higher authority. A *permissional society* recognizes that every citizen has been granted the same permission by the same higher authority. A *permissional society* does not mean that everyone does what they want when they want to. Let's repeat that last sentence. A *permissional society* does not mean that everyone does what they want when they want to. Therefore *permissional* is not to be confused with *permissive*. By no means is a permissional society a religious free-for-all. How does a permissional society function without chaos?

## KINGS AND PRIESTS

You are a king according to scripture, but there is a greater King – Jesus Christ. He is King of kings (1Timothy 6:15; Revelation 17:14; 19:16). Your kingdom and my kingdom must be fully submitted to His Kingdom, otherwise we are anarchist and rebellious.

We must continuously submit our kingdoms to His. This is done by daily confessing His lordship over our lives. The strength of our confession comes from what we believe in our hearts. If I truly believe my confession – that He is Lord – then I am willing to take up my cross daily and follow Him – regardless of my personal cost (Luke 9:23; 14:26-35).

The purpose of His Kingdom must be the purpose of your kingdom and my kingdom. He did not entrust us with a kingdom to function separate from His. Yes, we are expected to be productive with our kingdom, but that productivity is for His glory and not our gain (John 15:16).

How then can His Kingdom have any order when every citizen is a king and permitted to pursue the expansion of his or her kingdom? Such would be impossible if we fail to understand that a permissional society is brought into balance by obedience and accountability. Obedience and accountability can only function in an atmosphere of *mutual submission*. I must first commit myself to obey every instruction I receive from the Word of God and the Holy Spirit. My sphere of kingdom rule must be totally submitted to Jesus Christ, and I must also be submitted to you.

The same applies to you. You too must first obey every command of Jesus Christ. You must submit your sphere of kingdom rule under the authority of Jesus Christ, so that it can be a valuable asset to other 'kings' in the Lord's Kingdom. Our only purpose is to insure that Jesus Christ is glorified and His Kingdom is advanced. In the earth, our individual kingdoms must serve to advance the work of other kings in the Lord's Kingdom.

> *For though I be free from all [men], <u>yet have I made myself servant unto all</u>, that I might gain the more. (1Corinthians 9:19)*

> *For, brethren, ye have been called unto liberty; only <u>use not liberty for an occasion to the flesh, but by love serve one another</u>. (Galatians 5:13)*

> *<u>Submit yourselves to every ordinance</u> of man for the Lord's sake: whether it be to the king, as supreme; Or unto governors, as unto them that are sent by him for the punishment of evildoers, and for the praise of them that do well. For so is the will of God, that with well doing ye may put to silence the ignorance of foolish men: As free, and <u>not using your liberty for a cloke of maliciousness, but as the servants of God</u>. (1Peter 2:13-16)*

I am an apostle. I have been entrusted with a realm of authority (or kingdom) by the revelation Jesus Christ has given to me. Your kingdom may differ from mine. Yet the revelation you have from Jesus Christ is accompanied by the authority to advance it. Our individual kingdoms must find a place of mutual submission to each other for the glory of the Lord. If there is a clash between my kingdom and yours, it means that one or both of us are not in obedience or submitted to the King of kings. Conflicts are proof that one or both of us have placed our own kingdom above His. Quarrels imply that we have lost sight of His purpose in the earth.

The permissional society fails when individuals become self serving. It is diluted when the desire for personal glory takes preeminence over Divine Will. The Holy Spirit works through each of us accomplishing the purposes of God in the earth. If each of us accurately hear and obey the Holy Spirit, there would be no conflicts among us. However, we know that as humans our flesh from time to time will get in the way. So how is this handled?

## ACCOUNTABILITY IN THE HOUSE

Believers who try to 'go it alone' will eventually get into trouble. God did not design us or His church to operate in isolation. A permissional society does not mean a person has the right to *do their own thing* outside of interaction with other believers. The small gathering of believers in the house church provides the first layer of accountability that helps to eliminate isolationism and error. In addition, these small gatherings provide a safe environment for a believer to express what they believe their assignment is from the Lord. The other believers then have the opportunity to pray with them and give advice.

> But exhort one another daily, while it is called To day; lest any of you be hardened through the deceitfulness of sin. (Hebrews 3:13)

It has been mentioned before that there are several 'one-another' scriptures. In addition to loving one another, edifying one another, comforting one another and bearing one another's burdens, there is also the instruction to exhort one another. In Hebrews 3:13, we are instructed to exhort one another daily. Failure to do so could lead to one's heart becoming hardened through the deceitfulness of sin. The Amplified Bible specifically states that daily exhortation helps to keep one from entering into 'settled rebellion'.

The Greek verb translated *exhort* is *parakeleo*. This word is very similar to the Greek noun *parakletos* which is used as an adjective to describe the Holy Spirit as the *comforter*. Both words give the suggestion of one coming along side another person. The *parakeletos* or *comforter* comes along side a person to aid. It also was used for one who pleaded another's cause, an advocate or intercessor. The verb *parakeleo* or *exhort* means to come along side another to urge them to pursue a certain course of conduct, always looking to the future.[5]

In a permissional society, where a believer is free to pursue their assignment from God, exhortation is an important factor. To have someone '*come along side*' a believer and urge them to pursue a certain course of conduct implies a relational closeness that serves to protect them from slipping into error. One passage clearly states that exhorting should take place when believers gather (Hebrews 10:25). I believe this is the small intimate setting of believers gathering in homes.

In a permissional society, we must never lose sight of the two-fold aspect of our purpose. We must first be fully submitted to the Lord Jesus Christ and His purpose to establish God's Kingdom in the earth. And second, we must always remember that whatever we are assigned to do is to bring Him glory by being an asset to other believers in their quest to bring God glory through their assignment. Whatever my assignment is from God is to be strength to you. Whatever your assignment is from God is to be strength to me. Collectively our assignments help accomplish His purposes and bring Him glory.

Now let us turn our attention to those specifically entrusted with the oversight of the local church – the elders.

# No Longer Elders As Usual    8

From Genesis 50:7 when first mentioned in scripture to Revelation 19:4 when the twenty four elders fell down and worshipped God, elders have played an intricate role throughout biblical history. Over 175 times, elders, both good and bad are mentioned in scripture. Before there was a New Testament church, there were elders.

The Old and New Testament confirm the fact that a plurality of elders is God's form of government. In the Old Testament elders governed the nation (Exodus 24:1; Numbers 22:7). In the New Testament they governed cities and churches (Acts 14:23; Titus 1:5). There is never a lone elder over a church, city or nation. There was always a plurality of elders. The purpose of this plurality is to provide safety and accountability. Plurality greatly minimizes the potential of a dictatorship.

## THE SET MAN

Those who are proponents of the 'one pastor – one church' system usually point to Moses, Joshua, David and Solomon in the Old Testament and Paul and James in the New Testament. But a close look at these men quickly dissolves the idea of one man rule.

> *And Moses spake unto the LORD, saying, Let the LORD, the God of the* <u>*spirits of all flesh, set a man over the congregation,*</u> *Which may go out before them, and which may go in before them, and which may lead them out, and which may bring them in; that the congregation of the LORD be not as sheep which have no shepherd. And the LORD said unto Moses, Take thee Joshua the son of Nun, a man in whom is the spirit, and lay thine hand upon him; And set him before Eleazar the priest, and before all the congregation; and give him a charge in their sight. And thou shalt put some of thine honour upon him, that all the congregation of the children of Israel may be obedient. And he shall stand before Eleazar the priest, who shall ask counsel for him after the judgment of Urim before the LORD: at his word shall they go out, and at his word they shall come in, both he, and all the children of Israel with him, even all the congregation. And Moses did as the LORD commanded him: and he took Joshua, and set him before Eleazar the priest, and before all the congregation: And he laid his hands upon him, and gave him a charge, as the LORD commanded by the hand of Moses. (Numbers 27:15-23)*

Moses failed God at the waters of Meribah. He was forbidden the pleasure of entering the Promised Land. He had been the visionary for Israel for nearly forty years, but had lost the privilege of entering

Canaan for striking the rock in anger twice rather than speaking to it as he was commanded (Numbers 20:7-12). Moses wisely petitioned God for a successor. He asked God to set a man before the congregation so they would not be as 'sheep with no shepherd'. Of course we know that God chose Joshua for the task.

Moses and Joshua were given the vision and strategies for Israel's deliverance (Psalms 103:7; Joshua 1:5). But scripture clearly shows that both men relied on the elders of the nation.

> *And Moses and Aaron went and gathered together all the elders of the children of Israel: (Exodus 4:29)*

> *And the LORD said unto Moses, Go on before the people, and take with thee of the elders of Israel; and thy rod, wherewith thou smotest the river, take in thine hand, and go. (Exodus 17:5)*

> *And Moses came and called for the elders of the people, and laid before their faces all these words which the LORD commanded him. (Exodus 19:7)*

> *And the LORD said unto Moses, Gather unto me seventy men of the elders of Israel, whom thou knowest to be the elders of the people, and officers over them; and bring them unto the tabernacle of the congregation, that they may stand there with thee. (Numbers 11:16)*

> *And Joshua rose up early in the morning, and numbered the people, and went up, he and the elders of Israel, before the people to Ai. (Joshua 8:10)*

> *And Joshua gathered all the tribes of Israel to Shechem, and called for the elders of Israel, and for their heads, and for their judges, and for their officers; and they presented themselves before God. (Joshua 24:1)*

*And the people served the LORD all the days of Joshua, and all the days* *of the elders that outlived Joshua, who had seen all the great works of the* *LORD, that he did for Israel. (Judges 2:7)*

David served Israel as it's king. Because of his absolute rule as king, one could easily conclude that he was a one man ruler. But biblical evidence contradicts this idea.

*So all the elders of Israel came to the king to Hebron; and king David* *made a league with them in Hebron before the LORD: and they anointed* *David king over Israel. (2Samuel 5:3)*

*So David, and the elders of Israel, and the captains over thousands, went* *to bring up the ark of the covenant of the LORD out of the house of* *Obededom with joy. (1Chronicles 15:25)*

*And David lifted up his eyes, and saw the angel of the LORD stand* *between the earth and the heaven, having a drawn sword in his hand* *stretched out over Jerusalem. Then David and the elders [of Israel, who* *were] clothed in sackcloth, fell upon their faces. (1Chronicles 21:16)*

It is clear to see in scripture that even those who appeared to be one man rulers, were in fact visionaries who set forth the purposes of God through the elders (1Kings 8:1; 2Kings 6:32). This principle extended into the New Testament church.

## ELDERS AND CHURCH GOVERNMENT

Elders are appointed in the church to govern. Their role is to protect the flock of God from error, encroachment by wolves, and internal conflicts. God's idea to establish His Kingdom in the earth is the focus of their protective ministry. They serve to strengthen the ministry of others within the church. Elders are entrusted with the oversight of the local church, but they are not the Head of the church. Jesus Christ is the only Head of His Church. Let's see how elders function in this environment.

## JESUS CHRIST, THE ONLY HEAD OF THE CHURCH

Jesus is Lord. He is the head of His Church. He is the head of the government of His Church. He is the King over His kingdom. He rules as a righteous king. He is reigning now (1Corinthians 15:25; Ephesians 1:22; Colossians 1:18). He does not rule by public opinion polls, nor does He campaign for re-election. In His government, there is no voting. His word is the law by which everyone in His kingdom lives. Formally, His government is a theocracy. In basic terms, He decides – we do.

To some a theocracy would appear to be a dictatorship. That is far from the truth. Jesus rules over a unique kingdom wherein every citizen is a king, and every citizen is a priest (1Peter 2:9; Revelation 1:6; 5:10). He rules over a kingdom wherein every citizen has been given a kingdom with corresponding authority (Matthew 16:19; Luke 12:32; Romans 5:17; 2Corinthians 10:13). He rules a kingdom where submission and servanthood are the foundation of authority (Matthew 20:25-28; Mark 9:35; Ephesians 5:21). The nature of this kingdom is *permissional.*

## JESUS CHRIST, THE SERVANT LEADER

I have been involved in several traditional church ordinations, both in the United States and abroad. The candidates for ordination were brought before the congregation and given a solemn charge to 'preach the word in and out of season' (2Timothy 4:2). Then the other officiants and I laid hands on them, and before the people they were *'elevated'* to a position of ministry. That's the way I was ordained, and I assumed it was to be the same for everyone else. However, I have now come to understand that the concept of *elevating* someone into ministry does not line up with Jesus Christ who is the ultimate example of ministry leadership.

> *Who hath believed our report? and to whom is the arm of the LORD revealed? For he shall grow up before him as a tender plant, and as a root out of a dry ground: he hath no form nor comeliness; and when we shall see him, there is no beauty that we should desire him. He is despised and rejected of men; a man of sorrows, and acquainted with grief: and we hid as it were our faces from him; he was despised, and we esteemed him not (Isaiah 53:1-3)*

It amazes me that Jesus Christ, as a man in the earth, did not have the physical attributes that made Him stand out in a crowd. There are no scriptures that describe how our Lord looked. The passage above from Isaiah is only a prophetic glimpse of what was to be expected of Him. Even Saul, the Old Testament king and David his successor were reported to be handsome men (1Samuel 9:2; 16:12). Too often, a person's looks are used as measuring tools for their leadership skills. David in fact did fairly well, but Saul was a dismal failure.

> *Let this mind be in you, which was also in Christ Jesus: Who, being in the form of God, thought it not robbery to be equal with God: But made himself of no reputation, and took upon him the form of a servant, and was made in the likeness of men: And being found in fashion as a man, he*

*humbled himself, and became obedient unto death, even the death of the cross. Wherefore God also hath highly exalted him, and given him a name which is above every name: That at the name of Jesus every knee should bow, of things in heaven, and things in earth, and things under the earth; And that every tongue should confess that Jesus Christ is Lord, to the glory of God the Father. (Philippians 2:5-11)*

If we follow the leadership example of our Lord, it is clear that humility and servitude was His nature. Jesus is the Son of God (Matthew 16:16), yet He entered the earth as a servant, fully obedient to His Father – even to death. His 'sonship' was His highest calling, yet He was known as the Son of Man willing to wash the feet of His followers (Matthew 20:28; John 13:14).

Every believer is called to be a son (John 1:12; 1John 3:1). This intimate relationship with the Father should be cherished above all. Being a son takes precedence over any ministry assignment. Too often the focus is towards 'being' something in ministry. But when Jesus ordained His disciples, it was not a promise for ministry, but a call to be with Him (Mark 3:14KJV). A call to ministry is not so much an elevation as it is a trust being placed in a believer by the Lord. It is an opportunity for a believer to serve the Body of Christ (Ephesians 4:1-2; 1Corinthians 1:26).

*For I am the least of the apostles, that am not meet to be called an apostle, because I persecuted the church of God. But by the grace of God I am what I am: and his grace which was bestowed upon me was not in vain; but I laboured more abundantly than they all: yet not I, but the grace of God which was with me. (1Corinthians 15:9-10)*

*Whereof I was made a minister, according to the gift of the grace of God given unto me by the effectual working of his power. Unto me, who am less than the least of all saints, is this grace given, that I should preach among the Gentiles the unsearchable riches of Christ; (Ephesians 3:7-8)*

Paul often expressed his humility in being called as an apostle. It is clear that he did not consider being called as an apostle an elevation. Although he never personally walked with Jesus, he demonstrated what Jesus taught His disciples about leadership:

- To serve rather than be served (Matthew 23:11; Acts 20:33-35)

- To live sacrificially for others (John 15:12-13; 1Corinthians 9:14-18)

- To have compassion (Mark 6:34; Galatians 4:19)


## ELDERS 'SHOULDER' THE RESPONSIBILITY OF THE CHURCH

Elders are the entrusted authorities to govern God's idea to establish His Kingdom in the earth through His church. Not as lords, but as servants and examples.

*For unto us a child is born, unto us a son is given: and the government shall be upon his shoulder: and his name shall be called Wonderful, Counsellor, The mighty God, The everlasting Father, The Prince of Peace (Isaiah 9:6)*

Isaiah 9:6 declares that 'the government shall be upon his shoulder'. The shoulder is a part of the body. To me this implies that although He is the Head of His government, He yet entrusts some of it to His Body –

the Church. You cannot read the New Testament without becoming aware of the fact that not only is there government, but also there are those entrusted with carrying out various aspects of His government. These individuals are not lords, but rather servants entrusted with responsibilities that protect the building of the Lord's church in the earth. These are the elders of the church.

## ELDERS MUST BE QUALIFIED

Elders are not just older men evolving from among a group of believers. They are not just the 'most mature' in a group. Elders must be proven by the Word of God. Scripture outlines spiritual, character, domestic and ministry qualifications. Overlooking or ignoring these qualifications will bring great damage to the church.

Gene A. Getz gives an historical glimpse of why Paul outlined the need for specific qualifications for elders. His *Timeline Regarding Local Church Leadership* traces elders and church leadership from A.D. 45 to A.D. 68.[6] This valuable insight opens our understanding as to why certain qualifications were necessary for elders. He wrote:

> Paul viewed the position of being an "elder/overseer" as a very significant role, and anyone who had a desire to serve in this way would be pursuing a valuable, upright, and responsible ministry. However, Paul also made it unmistakably clear that a man who served in this position should demonstrate character qualities that reflect Christlike maturity. Apparently, some of the men who were already "elder/overseers"—perhaps some that Paul has exhorted in Miletus—were distorting "the truth in order to draw away disciples after them" (Acts 20:30).

However, there were obviously other men in Ephesus who also wanted to be spiritual leaders but who were definitely not demonstrating "noble character," disqualifying them from being involved in this "noble task" (1 Timothy 3:1).[7]

Dr. Kevin J. Connor thoroughly outlines the qualifications for elders in his book *The Church in the New Testament*.[8] As you read them, it will be clear that elders do not simply evolve, but that they are men who have been proven in spirituality, character, domestic lifestyles and ministry over a period of time. The following is a summary of these qualifications.

The Spiritual Qualifications

- An Elder must be born again (John 3:1-5)

- An Elder must have been baptized in water (Mark 16:15-20; Acts 2:37-47)

- An Elder must be baptized and filled with the Holy Spirit (Acts 2:1-4)

- An Elder must be made an overseer by the Holy Spirit (Acts 20:28)

The Character Qualifications (1 Timothy 3:1-11; Titus 1:6-16; 1 Peter 5:1-3)

- An Elder must be blameless, with unquestionable integrity

- An Elder must be orderly, disciplined and well behaved

- An Elder must be vigilant

- An Elder must be temperate, self-controlled

- An Elder must be sober-minded, sensible; not irrational

- An Elder must be just, righteous, impartial

- An Elder must be Holy, devout, pleasing God

- An Elder must be a lover of good

- An Elder must be hospitable, willing to receive into their homes

- An Elder must be patient, gentle, kind and considerate

- An Elder must not be quarrelsome, contentious, or a brawler

- An Elder must not be prone to anger or quick tempered

- An Elder must not be a striker, combative or violent

- An Elder must not be greedy of filthy lucre, or financial gain, or receiving money dishonestly

- An Elder must not be covetous, or idolatrous

- An Elder must not be self-willed, unwilling to work with others

- An Elder must not be given to wine

- An Elder must have a good reputation in and out of the church

- An Elder must be grave, serious

- An Elder must not be double-tongued, two-faced, or deceptive

- An Elder must not be a slanderer or liar

- An Elder must be faithful in all things, reliable, dependable and willing to go 'above and beyond' for the care of the church

- An Elder must be a good steward of personal and church resources

- An Elder must desire the office of an elder and be willing to qualify for it

- An Elder must not lord over God's people

- An Elder must be an example to the church

The Domestic Qualifications
- An Elder must rule his own house well

- An Elder must be the husband of one wife (not a bigamist or polygamist)

The Elder's wife can disqualify him from serving as an elder. Therefore,
- An Elder's wife must be grave, honorable and honest

- The Elder's wife must not be a slanderer, gossiper or carrier of false information

- The Elder's wife must be sober-minded, sensible, not irrational, able to maintain confidentiality

- An Elder's wife must be faithful, reliable, trustworthy

An Elder's children can damage and disqualify a man from serving as an elder. Therefore,
- An Elder's children must be in subjection

- An Elder's children must show respect and reverence

- An Elder's children must be faithful

- An Elder's children should not be riotous or unruly

Ministry Qualifications

- Although a man can desire to be an elder, he must also be called by the Holy Spirit (Acts 20:28)

- An Elder must hold fast the faithful Word as he has been taught

- An Elder must be able to teach the Word of God

- An Elder must be able to exhort and convince

- An Elder must not be a novice, or a new believer

- An Elder must be able and willing to shepherd the flock of God, including following the example of the Great Shepherd Jesus Christ who laid down His life for the sheep (John 10:11)

As you can see, none of the qualifications reflect the age of the elder. Age is implied in maturity, but the previously listed qualifications define the foundation of a mature elder. It would nearly be impossible for an elder to simply evolve from among a group of believers. The office of the elder is a serious one. It is too valuable to be left to chance. The strength and success of the New Testament church, as outlined in this book, rests on the ability of apostles to train and release biblically sound elders.

## PAUL RESPECTED THE ELDERS

Paul respected the elders in each of the churches he developed. His letters to the churches went through the local elders first who passed the information along to the local church. He clearly did not overlook the local eldership. He addressed the 'church of the Thessalonians' (1Thessalonians 1:1), but reminded them to know, esteem and honor those who were over them in the Lord (1Thessalonians 5:12-13). When Paul left Miletus, and came to Ephesus, he sent for the elders – not the whole church (Acts 20:17). His instructions to Titus was to ordain elders in every city (Titus 1:5). I believe Paul's letters to the various churches went first to the local eldership.

Elders are to protect the flock against those who take money from the saints and subvert whole houses (Titus 1:10-11). They had to watch out for wolves seeking to draw disciples after themselves (Acts 20:29-30). They had to be vigilant against those who would try and teach heresy (2Peter 2:1). Paul had even warned them not to receive anyone – himself included – who preached another gospel (Galatians 1:8). Thus, for Paul to bypass the elders in a city would have been a violation of the order he himself had established.

## ELDERS AND DECISION MAKING

How are decisions made in the New Testament church? Some advocate mutual consensus as the only way decisions should be made. Personally, I agree that arriving at a consensus is a biblical way to arrive at a decision. All believers should be willing to fast and pray and seek mutual agreement in matters concerning the local gathering. However, the fact remains that at times, someone may have to step up to the plate and make decisions in the absence of consensus. This is a responsibility of the elders.

## THE JERUSALEM COUNCIL

A dispute arose in the church regarding circumcision. Some Jews taught that without being circumcised, the Gentile believers could not be saved. This created such a stir that it was decided that Paul, Barnabas and others among them should go to Jerusalem to the Apostles and Elders to deal with this matter (Acts 15:1-6).

Before we go further with this story, we need to take note of three historical facts. First, there had been persecution in Jerusalem that scattered the saints, but the Apostles had remained in Jerusalem (Acts 8:1). The result of this scattering caused the church to expand throughout the regions. However, most of those who went forth only taught other Jews (Acts 11:19). Eventually, the Gospel of Jesus Christ made its way to the Greeks. When the apostles in Jerusalem heard of it, they sent Barnabas to investigate as far as Antioch (Acts 11:22-24).

Second, while all of this was happening, Saul was converted on the road to Damascus (Acts 9:1-9). The news of his miraculous conversion also spread throughout the region. Because of his past brutality against the saints, many feared him and did not trust his conversion (Acts 9:26). It was Barnabas who ventured to find Saul and bring him to Antioch – where he had been assigned by the Apostles in Jerusalem (Acts 11:25-26).

It is in Antioch that Saul's Jerusalem connection becomes clearer. A group of prophets from Jerusalem visited Antioch. Remember, it was the Apostles in Jerusalem who had sent Barnabas to Antioch. Because of the prophetic insight of Agubus regarding an impending famine, the disciples in Antioch decided to send relief to the church in Judea. They sent the relief to the *elders* by Barnabas and Saul (Acts 11:27-30).[9] Saul was serving with Barnabas and was most likely being mentored by him.

Third, upon their return from Jerusalem, the Holy Spirit set Barnabas and Saul apart for ministry (Acts 12:25; 13:1-3). Their work began to touch the lives of Gentiles throughout the region. Their ministry was negatively affected by individuals from Judea who tried to teach the new Gentile converts that they needed to be circumcised in order to be saved. There appears to have been no success in resolving this matter in Antioch. The decision was made to go back to Jerusalem for clarification. This brings us back to the Jerusalem council.

The Apostles in Jerusalem obviously trusted Barnabas when they sent him to Antioch. He found and connected with Saul. From Paul's writings, it is also clear that his behavior around the Apostles in Jerusalem garnered their respect for him, and that he respected them. However, Paul was emphatic that he was not subject to those who attempted to disrupt his ministry with legalism (Galatians 2:5). Implicit in the decision to go to Jerusalem was the issue of being subject to the authority of the apostles and elders there.

The final decision regarding circumcision of the Gentiles was made by James. His judgment pleased the apostles, elders and the whole church. Letters were sent by the 'apostles, elders and brethren' to the brethren of Antioch, Syria and Cilicia. Scripture states that they gathered the whole multitude together in Antioch. I believe this took place after the local elders had been notified first (Acts 15:30). The letter was sent to the brethren of Antioch, Syria and Cilicia who were most likely the elders (Acts 11:30).

I have given you much information to come to one conclusion – it was the elders in Jerusalem who made the final decision in this serious matter. The decision was not made by consensus at the local level. The apostles and elders in Jerusalem were sought out to consider and decide this matter.

Barnabas, Saul, and the Jews demanding circumcision all gave their views on the matter, but you can't get past the fact that James, an apostle and elder made the final decision. His decision apparently pleased and effected the church in Jerusalem, Antioch, Syria and Cilicia.

## ONE TIME BUT BIBLICAL

Some say that this was an isolated event. They don't believe the way they made this decision can be used as a working model today. I obviously disagree.

There are many 'one-time' events in scripture. However, just as the Old Testament provided types and shadows for the early church, the historical events of the early church provides us with insight to living according to scripture (Romans 15:4; 1Corinthians 10:11; 2Timothy 3:16). To invalidate an event because it only shows up once sets a dangerous precedence.

Consensus decision making is good. Yet, if consensus was the sole answer, Barnabas and Saul would have sought to resolve the matter of circumcision with the Judiazers over time. Instead, they sought out spiritual authorities who they trusted and were willing to submit themselves to for an answer.

This is significant. By going to Jerusalem to the apostles and elders, they put themselves in the position of having a judgment made against them. Thank God James made the decision he did. Barnabas and Saul did not know what the outcome would be when they went to Jerusalem. They simply submitted themselves to the Jerusalem council of apostles and elders.

## Decision Making In The 21st Century New Testament Church

Unfortunately, from time to time various conflicts will arise in the church. That is a reality we must be biblically prepared to handle. When people have differences and disagreements, decisions will have to be made. The devil would love to use these conflicts to destroy the work of the church. God in His wisdom has given us examples in His word to find Godly resolutions.

How can issues in the church be resolved today?

Let's begin with the house church gathering, the most foundational level of the Church. Even among this small group of believers, differences of opinions will occur. Confronting issues with prayer and open dialogue to arrive at a mutual consensus is the best way to resolve conflicts. But there may be times when a consensus cannot be reached. It is in times like this that those in the house church should '*call for the elders of the church*' to help them navigate through their conflict. This is why elders must be spiritually mature and impartial.

The elders do not necessarily have to make a decision for the group. They should provide fresh biblical insight to help them arrive at a consensus. However, if it appears to the elders that a resolution cannot be found, or if decisions by a particular house church had the potential of negatively affecting the whole church, then it is the elder's responsibility and scriptural right to make the decision they prayerfully believe is the best decision for all concerned.

Those effected by the decision are required by scripture to submit to the decision (Hebrews 13:17). Everyone may not agree with the elders, but everyone should respect the authority entrusted to them.

## FIVE RESPONSIBILITIES OF THE ELDER

An elder must be willing to lay down his life for those he serves. Being an elder is not a job. It is a lifelong commitment to care for God's people (John 10:11-15; 1John 3:16). Their function is not a placid one. With God's grace, they maintain the weight of caring for the church and have five primary responsibilities.

1.   The Responsibility of Ruling the Flock of God

The bible speaks of elders who rule in the church. Some have written and taught that this ruling is simply being an example to believers. One way of eliminating a thing is to redefine it. Whoever controls the language – controls the issue. We need to explore what it means for elders to rule in the church.

> One that ruleth well his own house, having his children in subjection
> with all gravity; (For if a man know not how to rule his own house, how
> shall he take care of the church of God?) (1Timothy 3:4-5)

Before a man can be considered for eldership, he must first past the test of 'ruling' his own house. The way he 'rules' his immediate house, including his wife and children, will have tremendous impact in his care of the church of God, or even if can qualify to do so.

The Greek word that was translated *rule* in the above scriptures is *proistemi*. It means *to stand before, to lead and to carefully and diligently attend to.* In two other scriptures *proistemi* is translated *maintain* (Titus 3:8, 14) and in another it is translated as *over* (1Thessalonians 5:12). In all cases there is the distinct connotation of being in the forefront, leading, caring and oversight.

Within the very basic qualifications for eldership, the concept of ruling is established. To redefine this as simply being an example greatly weakens the role of elders. At all times they must be an example to believers, but the pattern of elders ruling is continued throughout the New Testament.

To give you a better insight regarding this role of the elder, I have inserted all the words describing *proistemi* into the text of two common scriptures referring to elders.

<u>1Timothy 5:17</u>

Let the elders that [*stand before you, lead you, carefully and diligently attend to you, are over you, and maintain you*] well be counted worthy of double honour, especially they who labour in the word and doctrine.

<u>1Thessalonians 5:12-13</u>

And we beseech you, brethren, to know them which labour among you, and are [*standing before you, leading you, carefully and diligently attending to you, are over you, and maintaining you*] you in the Lord, and admonish you; And to esteem them very highly in love for their work's sake. And be at peace among yourselves.

## THE CONCEPT OF HIERARCHY

One misconception we must overcome is that of hierarchy. The responsibility of ruling is not hierarchal in nature but rather functional. In 1Thessalonians 5:13 we are taught to esteem them very highly *for their work's sake* – not for their titles. The church must understand their function, and learn to esteem them. These men are not super saints with spiritual superiority, but they have been given a sacred responsibility to care for the Church of God. Dr. Kevin Connor observed that, *"Although Elders are not perfect, yet they are God's established authorities over His people"*.[10]

> *Remember them which have the rule over you, who have spoken unto you the word of God: whose faith follow, considering the end of their conversation. (Hebrews 13:7)*

> *Obey them that have the rule over you, and submit yourselves: for they watch for your souls, as they that must give account, that they may do it with joy, and not with grief: for that is unprofitable for you. (Hebrews 13:17)*

In these passages from Hebrews, *rule* is translated from the Greek word *hegeomai*. It means to guide in a more authoritative sense. It can mean 'to lead' and 'to command' with official authority. Again, *rule* is more than just being an example.

First we are admonished to '*remember*' them who serve in this capacity. Later, we are told to 'obey' them that have the rule over us. In the first instance, '*to remember them that have rule*' is to take consideration of their lifestyle of faith and to imitate it. In other words, those who have rule must demonstrate a life of faith for others to follow. *Remember* implies being an example to believers, the word *rule* does not.

In the second instance, we are told to *obey* them that have rule over us. The word translated as obey is *peitho*. It means to be persuaded or convinced by. It means to rely upon. It is not a form of obedience that implies forced submission to authority, but to do so by persuasion. This kind of obedience is a result of someone trusting their leadership to watch for the well-being of their soul. It further makes it clear that the leader must give an account for their ministry to believers. Voluntary submission makes it possible for those ruling to do so with joy.

The end of this passage is the admonition that failure to obey and submit is *unprofitable*. This again implies a conflict caused by a person's failure to live within the framework of the governmental structure.

In every city there are prescribed traffic laws that are enforced by local police. Our responsibility is to obey the law and the local police. You do not fear the police as long as you obey the law. However, if you or I disobey the law, even in ignorance, it is the duty and responsibility of the police to make me aware of the infraction. An individual's response to the police can determine if they get a warning or end up in jail. Even the simplest infraction can escalate from a warning to time in jail if they refuse to cooperate with the police.

Likewise, the Word of God is our instruction for daily living. In the church, elders (as we will see later), are to insure that we understand how to live the Word. Elders encourage me to self govern myself in obedience to the Word of God. If I err, of course the first thing I should do is repent to the Lord Jesus Christ. But there may be times I do not know that my actions were in violation of the Word of God. If I am in covenant relationship with other believers, they may be able to show me my wrong.

When I am approached by an elder for correction, my response is important. A simple error can be corrected by the mature loving guidance of elders or I can escalate the matter into rebellion if I reject the instructions. The latter would be unprofitable for me, because the elders must protect the church.

## 2. The Responsibility of Protecting the Church

When Paul traveled through Miletus, he called for the elders in Ephesus. In his parting instructions to them he warned about wolves who would try and damage the church. He even said that some of these wolves may come from among their own ranks.

> *Take heed therefore unto yourselves, and to all the flock, over the which the Holy Ghost hath made you overseers, to feed the church of God, which he hath purchased with his own blood. For I know this, that after my departing shall grievous wolves enter in among you, not sparing the flock. Also of your own selves shall men arise, speaking perverse things, to draw away disciples after them. Therefore watch, and remember, that by the space of three years I ceased not to warn every one night and day with tears (Acts 20:28-31).*

Wolves are individuals who may at first seem like they are an acceptable part of the church. They are usually individuals seeking to create their own little kingdoms by drawing the innocent to themselves. Their purpose is never to build and edify, but rather to fleece the sheep for their own benefit. Wolves take financial, spiritual and emotional advantage of the weak. They creep into house churches and lead many astray (2Timothy 3:6).

All wolves are dangerous, but the most dangerous wolves are the ones that are known leaders within a local church. They have gained the trust of other leaders, as well as the flock. They use that trust to take advantage of the flock. Elders have the responsibility to protect the flock from these wolves.

3.  Elders Have The Responsibility To Teach Sound Doctrine

During the time I was writing this book, I received an email from a friend who was concerned about the doctrine of universalism and inclusion becoming popular in some house church circles. In each instance, these were isolated little groups without any elders or apostolic input. Such groups are open season for those who introduce heresies and false teachings (2Peter 2:1-2). Therefore, elders must be alert and ready to swiftly deal with doctrinal error to protect the hearts of those in the church (Ecclesiastes 8:11).

> *Holding fast the faithful word as he hath been taught, that he may be able by sound doctrine both to exhort and to convince the gainsayers. For there are many unruly and vain talkers and deceivers, specially they of the circumcision: Whose mouths must be stopped, who subvert whole houses, teaching things which they ought not, for filthy lucre's sake. (Titus 1:9-11)*

Paul instructed Titus to insure that elders hold to sound doctrine to refute those who attempt to introduce false doctrine. He specifically spoke against those of the circumcision who subvert whole houses (most likely house churches). Paul's instructions are specifically critical today.

Elders must understand sound doctrine, and be completely clear about the New Testament church structure. In this season of transition, there may be those from traditional church settings who may attempt to subvert those attending gatherings in houses in their area.

Subversion is the attempt to overturn or overthrow something from its foundation. It is corrupting or perverting by undermining morals, allegiance or faith. It is imperative that elders work tirelessly to insure that those embracing the New Testament church structure are given a sound biblical foundation.

On the other end of the spectrum, elders must also guard against those who are house, simple and organic church proponents who resist any church government that require submission to leaders. They too have the potential of subverting house church members by teaching a false freedom that implicitly eliminates the need for eldership (Romans 13:1; 2Peter 2:10).

## 4. Elders Have The Responsibility Of Overseeing The Flock

Oversight is only mentioned in relationship to elders. No where in scripture are five-fold ministry gifts instructed to oversee the local church. The role of elders is *governmental* whereas five-fold ministry gifts are *developmental*.

> *The elders which are among you I exhort, who am also an elder, and a witness of the sufferings of Christ, and also a partaker of the glory that shall be revealed: <u>Feed the flock of God which is among you, taking the oversight thereof</u>, not by constraint, but willingly; not for filthy lucre, but of a ready mind; (1Peter 5:1-2)*

> *And from Miletus he sent to Ephesus, and called the elders of the church...<u>Take heed therefore unto yourselves, and to all the flock, over the which the Holy Ghost hath made you overseers</u>, to feed the church of God, which he hath purchased with his own blood. (Acts 20:17 and 28)*

Three Greek words are used interchangeably in scriptures in relationship to elders. There is *presbuteros* (the elder), *episkopos* (bishop or overseer), and *poimen* (the shepherd). Biblically, all three words describe the same office or person. An elder, overseer and shepherd are one and the same, even though many institutional church systems have divided them into hierarchal positions. Scripturally, the term elder refers to the person, overseer is reference to the function and shepherd is often tied to the manner in which an elder does his work.

Elders must be generally aware of all that is occurring among the flock. We have already learned they must protect the flock from wolves and false doctrine, and they also need to be alert to conflicts among the flock. They need to monitor decisions being made that could affect the whole church. They should know the spiritual and material needs among the flock and anything that could impinge upon health of the church.

5. <u>Elders Have The Responsibility To Shepherd The Flock</u>

As we have already seen, shepherding (*poimen*) refers to the manner by which an elder does his work. Jesus Christ is the perfect example of being a good shepherd.

The first attribute of a good shepherd is his willingness to give his life for the sheep (John 10:11). Very few men today are put in a position where they need to give their physical life for those they care for. Nevertheless, elders must understand the level of sacrifice necessary to serve God's people.

A recent phenomenon has been the advent of the armor bearer. Some church leaders have surrounded themselves with those who carry their briefcases, fetch them water, drive them to events and even act as body guards to 'protect' them from the people. In my opinion, this is an affront to every principle of leadership found in scripture.

Jesus said that He came to serve, not to be served (Matthew 20:28; Luke 22:27). The greatest must be the servant (Matthew 23:11-12). Whoever exalts himself shall be abased (Luke 14:11). Yet, there are those who justify the opposite of Jesus' instructions on the basis of their perceived anointing. These people are hirelings at best (John 10:12-13), or worse they are false teachers who are making merchandise of God's people (2Peter 2:1-3).

Most infractions relating to elders are in the area of money. A good shepherd lives a sacrificial life. Instead of expecting the sheep to support them, they willingly give to provide for the flock. I am often amazed how some church leaders beguile people into giving to them by using scripture totally out of context (2Peter 3:16). Followers are told they will be blessed by 'blessing the man of God'. They are told that Psalms 133 is proof that when they bless the man at the top, that blessings will come down to them. That sounds more like trickle-down economics than scripture.

Paul openly taught about money. He taught that he should be able to receive financial support from those he ministered to, yet he refused to force them to give to him in order not to hinder the Gospel (1Corinthians 9:1-15). His concern for the Philippians was that fruit would abound to them (Philippians 4:10-19).

When he gathered the elders of Ephesus, he left no doubt that he had taken care of himself in ministry, and those who accompanied him. He said that he did this as an example to them, stating "...it is more blessed to give than receive". In other words, he expected elders to use their resources for the care of the flock, rather than expecting the flock to care for them (Acts 20:33-35).

An elder, as a shepherd is willing to give his life for the well-being of the sheep. An elder who does not approach his role sacrificially runs the risk of taking advantage of the church. Failure to do so disqualifies him in the eyes of the Lord.

> *So when they had dined, Jesus saith to Simon Peter, Simon, [son] of Jonas, lovest thou me more than these? He saith unto him, Yea, Lord; thou knowest that I love thee. He saith unto him, Feed my lambs. He saith to him again the second time, Simon, [son] of Jonas, lovest thou me? He saith unto him, Yea, Lord; thou knowest that I love thee. He saith unto him, Feed my sheep. He saith unto him the third time, Simon, [son] of Jonas, lovest thou me? Peter was grieved because he said unto him the third time, Lovest thou me? And he said unto him, Lord, thou knowest all things; thou knowest that I love thee. Jesus saith unto him, Feed my sheep. (John 21:15-17)*

> *The elders which are among you I exhort, who am also an elder, and a witness of the sufferings of Christ, and also a partaker of the glory that shall be revealed: Feed the flock of God which is among you, taking the oversight thereof, not by constraint, but willingly; not for filthy lucre, but of a ready mind; Neither as being lords over God's heritage, but being ensamples to the flock. And when the chief Shepherd shall appear, ye shall receive a crown of glory that fadeth not away. (1Peter 5:1-4)*

Peter learned directly from Jesus Christ the keys to being a good shepherd. When he admonished the elders in the above text, he instructed them to "feed the flock of God among them". This was the exact same instructions Jesus Christ had given him just prior to His ascension.

In John 21:15-17 as Jesus and the disciples dined, He turned and asked Peter a significant question. "Peter, do you love me more than these?" Of course Peter's answer was "Yes". Jesus then instructed him to feed His lambs. Twice more Jesus asked Peter the same question, and each time Peter answered the same, and three times Jesus instructed Peter to feed His sheep.

Most people focus on the instructions to 'feed Jesus sheep'. That is important, but what we often overlook is Jesus primary question, "Do you love me?" You cannot love God's people until you first love the Lord. An elder's shepherding ministry is a reflection of his love for Jesus Christ. Elders are shepherds. If they are to be examples to the flock they oversee, they must first follow the example of the Chief Shepherd, Jesus Christ.

## THE APOSTOLIC APPOINTMENT OF ELDERS

Elders do not simply evolve. They don't just appear. They just don't magically show up in their role. Elders in the early church were developed, trained and appointed by Apostles (Acts 14:23; Titus 1:5). The present transition taking place in the church will require input and direction from contemporary apostles who understand what is taking place in the earth (Ephesians 3:5). The next chapter will explore the important relationship the apostles and other five-fold ministers have with the elders and the church.

Mature elders are crucial to insuring that contemporary New Testament churches remain strong and vibrant. This chapter has covered many of the qualifications that an apostle would look for in a man to appoint him as an elder.

It is generally accepted by most biblical scholars that elders are appointed by apostles. This is a life long appointment that can only be broken by death or the sin of the elder (1Timothy 5:17-21). But what happens when the church multiplies and there may not be an apostle to appoint additional elders for the growing church?

> Thou therefore, my son, be strong in the grace that is in Christ Jesus. And the things that thou hast heard of me among many witnesses, the same commit thou to faithful men, who shall be able to teach others also. (2Timothy 2:1-2)

> But continue thou in the things which thou hast learned and hast been assured of, knowing of whom thou hast learned them; (2Timothy 3:14)

Paul's letter to Timothy touched the issue of perpetuity. He recognized that he would not always be physically available to teach and instruct, so he encouraged Timothy to commit all he had learned to faithful men, who in turn would be able to teach others. He further instructed Timothy to continue in the things he had learned. These instructions provide the groundwork for the perpetual growth and vibrancy of the church. The responsibilities taught in this chapter serve as a good barometer to measure the effectiveness of elders who have been appointed.

I believe that the initial elders of the local church should be trained and appointed by apostles. As the church grows, I believe those elders will have the strong, biblical foundation to seek out and appoint additional elders as the need arises. The physical presence of an apostle may not be possible at the time the appointment is made, yet the apostolic foundation laid by the apostle is essential for elders to build upon (1Corinthian 3:10-15).

# No Longer
# Five-Fold Ministry Gifts As Usual

9

Elders provide oversight and protection to the church. The nature of their role is *governmental*. The church must always grow and mature. For that the Lord Jesus Christ gave five gifts to His church – the apostle, the prophet, the evangelist, the pastor and the teacher – often referred to as the five-fold ministry gifts or the ascension gifts. They were given to bring the church to maturity; to the fullness of Christ Jesus (Ephesians 4:11-16). Their role is to develop the saints.

Both elders and five–fold ministry gifts are leaders, but the nature of their work is different. Whereas elders are *governmental* in nature, five-fold ministry gifts are *developmental* in nature. Failure to understand the difference in nature perpetuates the dysfunctional leadership model currently in most churches.

Our common church structure paradigm has been the 'one pastor one church model'. As the Lord began to restore the apostle and prophet back into the church, it was natural to try and plug these five ascension gifts into the structural model we have known and understood. We have tried to make five-fold ministry gifts function in a model different from what is seen in the New Testament. We have made them governmental, hierarchal, and created spiritual pecking orders that are completely unbiblical. This chapter takes a fresh look at each of these powerful gifts and how they were designed to bless and build the Body of Christ.

## ARE FIVE-FOLD MINISTRY GIFTS ELDERS?

This is an important question that must be addressed. There are two schools of thought in this matter.

*Five-fold ministers equip saints for the work while elders govern the saints in the work*

One view is that anyone called into one of the five-fold ministry gifts is also an elder in the church. The other view is that a person may be called into one of the five-fold ministry gifts, but that such does not automatically make them an elder. I personally believe the latter.

Remember, the elders are often appointed by apostles. Apostles are one of the five-fold ministers, but also the only one of the gifts clearly linked to eldership as we will discuss later. None of the requirements to be an elder include any of the attributes of the five-fold ministry gifts or vice versa. That would be a plus, but Paul never made being a prophet, evangelist, pastor or teacher a prerequisite for eldership. Twice in scripture we see that an elder or a servant must be "apt to teach" (1Timothy 3:2; 2Timothy 2:24). This kind of teaching stems from a readiness of the individual to instruct. It is not necessarily the ascension gift of the Teacher.

An elder can simultaneously function as one of the five-fold gifts to the church. Yet, because a person is called by Jesus Christ to serve in one of the five–fold ministry gifts, it does not automatically make them an elder. Although lines of service and ministry may cross, it is important that we keep the distinctions of *government* and *development* separate. This is important because elders and five-fold ministers must work together for the benefit of the church. They both serve as leaders, but the nature of their work and leadership is different. Five-fold ministers equip saints *for the work* while elders govern the saints *in the work*.

## JESUS IS BUILDING HIS CHURCH

The Church belongs to Jesus Christ. He shed His blood for her (Acts 20:28). He takes sole responsibility for building His church (Matthew 16:18). The Church is not built by denominations, or simple, organic or house church groups. The Church cannot be built upon programs, events or the popularity of a man. The Church is not being built for man. The Church is being built for the purposes of God alone (Ephesians 3:10; 5:25-27).

Like many, I developed a *mission statement* or a *church vision*. I was taught that to build an effective church, I had to have a clear vision. Generally speaking a vision statement is not wrong. However, I have come to realize that a vision statement can at times be a humanistic substitute when your spirit has not understood, or embraced the purposes of God (Matthew 13:11; Mark 4:11).

There is no vision other than God's. His vision is not contingent upon human ingenuity and efforts. Jesus Christ is in full control of the work being done in His church. It is a church that is systematically making the enemies of God His footstool (Acts 2:35; Hebrews 1:13; 10:12-13). When the enemies of God are fully subdued, Jesus will then deliver the Kingdom to God (1Corinthians 15:24-28).

The Church is vital to the Lord's work in the earth. That is why our vision must be His vision. Too often, our vision gives us the basis for bragging rights. The Church Jesus is building has no place for our pride. It is His church, and all glory belongs to Him. How then is Jesus building His church?

*And I say also unto thee, That thou art Peter, and upon this rock I will build my church; and the gates of hell shall not prevail against it. (Matthew 16:18)*

*And he gave some, apostles; and some, prophets; and some, evangelists; and some, pastors and teachers; For the perfecting of the saints, for the work of the ministry, for the edifying of the body of Christ: Till we all come in the unity of the faith, and of the knowledge of the Son of God, unto a perfect man, unto the measure of the stature of the fulness of Christ: That we henceforth be no more children, tossed to and fro, and carried about with every wind of doctrine, by the sleight of men, and cunning craftiness, whereby they lie in wait to deceive; But speaking the truth in love, may grow up into him in all things, which is the head, even Christ: From whom the whole body fitly joined together and compacted by that which every joint supplieth, according to the effectual working in the measure of every part, maketh increase of the body unto the edifying of itself in love. (Ephesians 4:11-16)*

Jesus declared to His disciples that He would build His Church upon the revelation of who He is (Matthew 16:18; 1Corinthians 12:3; Philippians 2:9-11). His Church would be built with lively stones who have a revelation *of* Him, rather than by religious people who just have information *about* Him (Ephesians 2:19-22; 1Peter 2:5). Thus, His plan requires that Christ be formed in every member of His Church (Romans 8:29; Ephesians 1:15-23; Galatians 4:19; Colossians 1:27).

The formation of Christ in each of us begins when we submit to the Lordship of Jesus Christ (John 1:12; 1John 3:1). Our next step is the choice to become a disciple of the Lord Jesus Christ. The invitation by Jesus Christ to *"deny yourself, take up your cross daily and follow me"* is given to every believer. (Luke 9:23-24; 14:25-27, 33). The decision to become a disciple is an individual choice. Discipleship is a total commitment. Jesus will not build His Church with those who fail to commit everything to Him.

Disciples draw strength from each other. There are over fifty verses in the New Testament that teach us how to minister to one another. The believers who gather in homes is the best place to admonish one another (Romans 15:14), exhort one another (Hebrews 10:25), edify one another (1Thessalonians 5:11) and of course love one another (John 13:35).

Disciples however, are not designed to simply be strong Christians per se. They are the building blocks through which Jesus will build His Church to accomplish the purposes of God in the earth (Romans 8:28; 2Timothy 1:9). Therefore, disciples need to be equipped for the tasks before them. This brings us back to the five-fold ministry gifts which were given to the Church by Jesus Christ to perfect or equip the saints for the work of ministry.

## THE WORK OF MINISTRY

After forty days of ministry following His resurrection, Jesus ascended back to heaven to sit on the right hand of the Father (Acts 1:3, 9-11; Romans 8:34). As He ascended, He gave gifts to men. These gifts are apostles, prophets, evangelist, pastors and teachers (Ephesians 4:9-11). Each gift was given a specific function to perfect or mature the saints for the work of ministry.

*The work of ministry is rooted in divine purpose and manifested through various tasks. If a task is not being done to accomplish God's purposes, then it becomes a mundane religious duty*

We must be careful not to define the *work of ministry* to tasks we perform in the church as we know it today. Keep in mind that when Paul referenced the 'work of ministry', ushering, singing in the choir, running sound equipment or working in the nursery did not exist. The work of ministry is much more than these. In today's current church structure they may be valuable 'helps' but they do not constitute the 'work of ministry'. The work of ministry is tasks done specifically for the benefit of God's purpose. Otherwise our work is no more than mundane religious activity.

The Holy Spirit is in the earth executing the purposes of God through obedient men and women. The Holy Spirit gives spiritual gifts, or divine enablement to these men and women. Through one individual He imparts the gift of prophecy, while through another He provides hospitality to the saints. One may be gifted to teach, while another is used to provide resources. The giving of these gifts is all the work of the Holy Spirit (1Corinthians 12:4). The gifts are given for the intent of fulfilling the purposes of God in the earth (1Corinthians 12:6; 15;28).

The five-fold ministry gifts Jesus gave to His church are the 'mentors' or 'trainers' that insure that the gifts of the Holy Spirit are utilized accurately. They serve to equip the saints for the work of ministry which is the ongoing fulfillment of God's purposes in the earth. The apostles, prophets, evangelists, pastors and teachers must work to insure that every believer they impact matures in their calling, purpose and ministry. This becomes a powerful cycle that perpetuates the Kingdom Mandate over and over again. Here's how:

> Five-fold ministers equip saints, who in turn, do the work of ministry which builds the Body of Christ, producing more saints, of which some will become five-fold ministers, who will equip saints, to do the work of ministry which will build the Body of Christ and produce more saints, of which some will become five-fold ministers, who will equip saints, to do the work of ministry which will build the Body of Christ and produce more saints, of which some will become five-fold ministers, who will equip saints, to do the work of ministry which will build the Body of Christ

I believe you get the point.

Dr. Greg Ogden has written one of the most detailed teachings regarding what it means to 'equip the saints'. In his book UNFINISHED BUSINESS[11], he skillfully breaks down the work of equipping the saints into three categories: (1) mending/restoring, (2) establish/lay foundations, and (3) prepare/train. I believe his insights are vital to understand the developmental nature of five fold ministers.

## RESTORING/MENDING

The first aspect of equipping is restoration and mending. There are three components of the restore/mend process. The first is to *fix what is broken*. The five-fold minister must be committed to the healing process necessary to bring a person back to wholeness. People often come to the Lord with worldly baggage. Their lives have been decimated by sin. Their souls are anemic and their relationships are often unhealthy.

The restoration and mending process begins immediately when a person submits their life to the Lordship of Jesus Christ. This is a sensitive process requiring much time. Some changes in a person's life will not happen over night. Therefore, a five-fold minister must be willing to invest time and energy into restoring and mending a broken life.

The second aspect is to *bring a person back in proper alignment*. The word sin means to 'miss the mark'. A life of sin is a life that is completely out of alignment with God and man. The more we yield to sin, the more out of alignment we become. The sad irony is that too often sin has been practiced so long that when righteousness is introduced, the righteous standard seems out of place (Isaiah 5:20; Romans 1:19-25).

Jesus taught that the way of holiness is narrow (Matthew 7:14). To align someone with the Word of God often requires the prayerful and skilful work of five-fold ministers. Alignment implies imposing restrictions that may not be comfortable, but that are necessary to bring a person into right standing with God (Galatians 4:1-2). It requires discipline and love to bring a person into a proper relationship with God (Ephesians 4:14-15). A person cannot be fit for the work of ministry unless they are properly aligned with the Lord.

The third aspect of restore/mend trilogy is *supplying what is lacking*. A new born baby does not have the understanding or physical capacity to prepare their own bottle. They soil their diapers and yet they have no ability to clean themselves. Likewise, new believers are like new babies. They generally do not know what things are healthy for their spirit man. They have not learned the value of developing solid relationships with other believers. When they make mistakes, they often run from the Lord rather than to Him. It is necessary for the five-fold minister to invest time, energy and resources to insure the spiritual health of the new believer. The ultimate goal is that every believer be healthy to do the work of ministry.

## ESTABLISH/LAY FOUNDATIONS

The second aspect of equipping according to Dr. Ogden is *establishing and laying foundations*. As I read his teaching in this area, I was reminded of Jeremiah 1:10:

> *See, I have this day set thee over the nations and over the kingdoms, to root out, and to pull down, and to destroy, and to throw down, to build, and to plant.*

The prophetic pattern Jeremiah described was to *root out*, which is to deny a plant its ability to absorb the necessary nutrients to live; to *pull down* – an act of dethroning; to *destroy* – which is to eliminate the possibility of ever existing again; and to *throw down* – to completely subdue. This opens the way to *build* (lay accurate foundations) and *to plant* (introduce new organisms that will grow naturally in this corrected environment). Often all the components required to equip a believer will flow simultaneously. In the process of restoring and mending, the five-fold minister will also be establishing the believer and laying a strong solid foundation within them.

The only foundation that can be established in a believer is Jesus Christ (1Corinthians 3:11; Ephesians 2:20). Paul travailed over the Galatians praying that Christ would be formed in them (Galatians 4:19). A major part of the equipping process is to insure that the saints have Jesus Christ as their source for everything. Notice, I did not say 'to have Jesus Christ at the center of all they do', but rather that Jesus Christ becomes the totality of their very existence. Jesus Christ cannot be reduced to being a partner in a saints activities; Jesus Christ must be the very life of the saint (Acts 17:28; Galatians 2:20; 1Peter 4:1-2).

How does a believer learn to allow Christ to be totality of their life? It begins with the Word of God. No program or event can replace allowing the Word of God to be engrafted (James 1:21). Once again the 'one anothering' that takes place in the house church setting serves to encourage believers to do more than simply '*know the Word*', but to strive to '*do the Word*' (Hebrews 10:24-25; James 1:22-25).

The five-fold minister recognizes that the Word of God is the primary source for direction and power. Therefore they will encourage the believer to obey the Word of God. The goal is to train the saints to rely on the Word of God and the Holy Spirit rather than become solely dependent on human direction (2Timothy 3:16-17; Hebrews 4:12). By both example and precept, the five–fold minister must instill the 'how-to's' of self governance and trusting covenant relationships. Those equipping will keep the person of Jesus Christ in the forefront by teaching the believers the importance of strict adherence to scripture. Therefore, sound doctrine is imperative. This leads to a major attribute of establishing and laying foundations.

In order to establish and lay foundations, the five-fold minister can most effectively equip the saints by modeling what they teach. Too often the church has allowed a '*do as I say—without me showing proof that I have done it myself*' form of leadership. Untested leaders have been loosed upon the church that teach and lead from theory rather than experience.

Thousands graduate from seminaries and somehow become experts in arenas they have never personally touched. Many teach 'discipleship classes' who have never been discipled themselves. To them, discipleship has been reduced to a religious bible study rather than the committed life Jesus expects (Luke 14:26-27).

Paul and Barnabas were used by the church in Jerusalem., Their recommendation for ministry came as a result of the recognition the local elders had of their lifestyle (Acts 15:25-26). Paul later wrote the churches at Corinth and Philippi to follow him as he followed Christ – because of his example (1Corinthians 11:1; Philippians 3:17). He taught Timothy to be an example to believers (1Timothy 4:12). Likewise, he taught Titus to show himself as a pattern of good works (Titus 2:7). He recognized His lifestyle had a profound effect on his ministry to others (1Corinthians 9:27; 2Timothy 3:10-11).

Those who are five-fold ministers must live all they teach. This is a crucial hour for the church. Leadership will not be able to hide behind titles and religious authority. If they are not living what they teach, they will be exposed and potentially disqualified from leading.

## Prepare/Train

The third aspect of equipping is that of preparation and training. Too often, this has been the sole focus of the church. We begin preparing and training new believers with little consideration of restoring, mending, establishing and laying foundations. Our efforts have been on what a believer *can do* rather than who he or she is *to become*. This has resulted in churches being led by immature, self-centered and character flawed individuals. We must never lose sight of the fact that in God's sight, *who you are is of more value than what you do.*

The phase of preparing and training is the last piece of the equipping trilogy. The idea of preparing and training is undergirded with components that test an individual's character and lifestyle.

The first thing that must be taught in the prepare/train component of equipping, is how to be a good steward of one's gifts and calling. Spiritual gifts are not toys. A calling is not an opportunity for self-promotion. Whatever God has entrusted you with is for His purposes, and His glory only. It is so sad to see how some have prostituted their gifts for the sake of money and fleshly glory. Five-fold ministers must model and teach the value of being a good steward over one's gift.

The second facet is to mobilize gifts into ministry teams. This provides accountability and maturing simultaneously. A team may be two or more persons ministering together. Jesus sent the disciples out in pairs (Luke 10:1). Paul traveled with many who ministered with him (Acts 19:29; 20:34).

Trained ministry teams will be important as churches transition to the New Testament model. Members of various ministry teams provide gifts that help to encourage and strengthen believers. Trained ministry teams will serve as inoculants to help strengthen the church and provide spiritual nutrients necessary to keep it healthy. Through prophecy, healing, teaching and more, ministry teams are vital to building the church (Matthew 1:7-8; Luke 10:7-9).

The final aspect of preparing and training is to 'provide specialized training' to develop ministry teams.

Years ago, the Lord instructed me to 'provide a viable outlet for all the ministry gifts'. The New Testament structure is the way this can be done accurately and effectively. Generally speaking, in the current church structure, ministry gifts are limited and performance based. Only a few have the opportunity to 'minister', and usually it's done during altar calls.

In the New Testament structure, a region may have several hundred house churches. Trained ministry teams will be able to minister from house to house in these relational small group settings. House church members will be energized by the spiritual input given by the ministry team. The ministry team members will mature as house church members affirm their gifts and ministry.

Specialized training is mandatory for anyone seeking to serve the Body of Christ on a ministry team. In chapter five I described the three-fold cord of the church consisting of the house church, the whole church and the temple. It is in the temple that much of the specialized training will take place. Those desiring to serve on ministry teams will need hands-on and classroom training.

The church is a permissional culture. Specialized training strengthens this unique culture. Training is designed to insure that there is consistency and continuity in the church. There is a lot of individual freedom in the New Testament structured church.

therefore it is necessary to provide focused training (Acts 19:8-9; 1Timothy 6:1-3; Titus 1:5; 2:1). Without clear preparation and training, the door is open for individuals to use their freedom as 'an occasion to the flesh' (1Corinthians 8:9; Galatians 5:13; 1Peter 2:16).

## THE FIVE-FOLD GIFTS

The five-fold ministry gifts are given to the church by Jesus Christ to equip the saints for the work of ministry. Each gift has a unique function. All five ascension gifts serve to mature the church (Ephesians 4:11-13).

In the New Testament model of the house church, whole church and temple, the five-fold ministers provide a significant role in the development of the saints. I will not attempt to add to the many authors who have thoroughly described the individual roles of each ministry gift. However, I will interject that most writers have applied these gifts to the current institutional church model. The following summary of each gift is written to remind you of the primary function of each gift as well as how they serve in the church model described in this book.

### Apostle

The apostle is a foundational gift to the church (Ephesians 2:20). The Greek word translated as apostle is *apostolos* meaning 'a sent one'. Watchmen Nee observed that apostles are not men of special gifts, but of special commission. It is their commission, not their spiritual gifts that sets them apart as apostles.[12]

Apostles are pioneers – not settlers. The nature of their commission is that of movement and not of being dormant. Apostles lay foundations, and leave the building to others (1Corinthians 3:10).

They establish, strengthen and encourage churches (Acts 15:41; 16:5). They establish doctrine (Acts 2:42; 1Timothy 1:3). They appoint elders, and leave them to care for the local church (Acts 14:23; 20:32; Titus 1:5)

Apostles are trans-local. They serve multiple *churches* – not just a single local church. Local elders oversee the local church, and apostles minister throughout the churches. No where in scripture do we find an apostle *over* a network of churches. Instead, apostles serve with the local elders in every place they are sent by the Holy Spirit. Therefore, because apostles are trans-local, it is important that local believers be equipped to discern true apostles (Revelation 2:2).

Apostles must seek out proven prophets, and mature prophets must bond with proven apostles. Together they form the synergy necessary to form the foundation of the New Testament church.

What is the relationship between apostles and elders? Apostles are the only one of the five ascension gifts *directly* linked to elders.

Peter wrote to the elders, and declared his eldership among them (1Peter 5:1). The Apostle John declared himself as an elder (3John 1:1). The Jerusalem council was a conclave of apostles and elders (Acts 15:2-6, 22-23; 16:4). Paul (an apostle) met with James (an apostle) and the elders of Jerusalem (Acts 21:15-18). There are no scripture that link prophets, evangelists and teachers to elders. This does not mean these gifts were not present, available or serving in the church.

As noted before, the pastor is indirectly linked to the elder. Implicit in scripture is that some pastors may also be elders. But scripture is clear that all apostles are elders.

The elders' primary role is that of *governing*, and the role of five-fold ministry gifts is that of *developing*. The apostle seems to fit into both categories. The apostle both governs and equips. To understand the apostles' role better we must again remember that the church is both global and local. Apostles are elders in the global church, whereas elders serve the local church. Apostles are subject to the elders of the local church. He can sit with them as a peer, not as their overseer. No where in scripture do you find the apostles asserting absolute rule over local churches. Yet, the local elders should respect apostles and consider their spiritual advice and counsel (1Corinthians 9:2; 2:12).

> *And God hath set some in the church, first apostles, secondarily prophets, thirdly teachers, after that miracles, then gifts of healings, helps, governments, diversities of tongues. (1Corinthians 12:28)*

Some teach that the above passage implies a hierarchal ranking of various ministry gifts. They believe that apostles are ranked first, followed by prophets, teachers and so on. However, this passage fails to include the pastor and the evangelist. Why would Paul leave them out of this list?

The answer is that Paul was not giving a top–down hierarchal list of ministry gifts as some have suggested. His focus was on what God has set in the church to make it healthy. A pivotal verse is first Corinthians 12:25.

*That there should be no schism in the body; but that the members should have the same care one for another.*

Paul's concern was that the body be healthy which is accomplished through mutual care for one another. He then lists components of a healthy body. If you focus on the numerical adjectives *first, secondarily and thirdly*, you will conclude that Paul is only discussing ministry rank. If your focus is on the *apostle, prophet, teacher, miracle (workers)*, etc., then you see that he is emphasizing functions in the body. This becomes evident when he asks, "Are all apostles? Are all prophets? Are all teachers?" The clear answer to these questions is "no". Apostles are first because they are foundational. You begin building the foundation *first*. That is nature of the apostle's function to the church.

Finally, Paul encourages the Corinthian believers to gravitate towards the best gifts (1Corinthians 12:31). The best gifts are rooted in mutual care, submission and love – not hierarchal positioning.

Prophets
Prophets and prophetess are called with the other five-fold ministers to equip the saints. Their ministry is to speak the mind of the Lord for the benefit of the church. Like the apostle, the prophet is a foundational gift. Several scriptures link the prophet with the apostle.

*Therefore also said the wisdom of God, I will send them prophets and apostles, and [some] of them they shall slay and persecute: (Luke 11:49)*

*And are built upon the foundation of the apostles and prophets, Jesus Christ himself being the chief corner [stone]; (Ephesians 2:20)*

It is the eternal wisdom of God that apostles and prophets be closely linked as He builds His church. Unfortunately, because of our hierarchal mindsets, the apostles and prophets have often become separate and exclusive of each other. This was not the Lord's intent.

Apostles must seek out proven prophets, and mature prophets must bond with proven apostles. Together they form the synergy necessary to form the foundation of the New Testament church.

When God called Moses (an apostolic type), to lead Israel out of Egypt, He established Aaron as his prophet because Moses claimed he was inarticulate (Exodus 4:10-18; 7:1). Aaron was Moses' prophet. Moses had God's plan, but Aaron articulated it (Psalms 103:7). Aaron spoke the desires of God, as he received it from Moses. This is important to understand.

I am not implying that prophets cannot speak from what they receive directly from God. Apostles and prophets need to build trust in each other so that apostolic building and prophetic utterances are unified. Too often there is subtle conflict between the two creating a schism in the Body of Christ. What would have happened to Israel if Aaron, as the prophet, had spoken something totally different from Moses? Yet, this is what happens too often in the church. Apostles have their own ministries going in one direction, and prophets have their own ministries going in another direction – and the two often fail to meet. The apostolic/prophetic foundation is cracked and the church building is flawed.

Scripture specifically instruct prophets to be subject to others (1Corinthians 14:32). Believers are taught to test all spirits to see if they are of God. The implication is that false spirits can be introduced by prophets (1John 4:1). All ministry workers should submit to each other. But this is especially true for apostles and prophets. They must know each others' function and be willing to submit to each other for the glory of God.

Prophecy edifies the church (1Corinthians 14:4). Scripture teaches that 'all may prophesy' (1Corinthians 14:31). God's Spirit has and is being poured out on all flesh resulting in 'sons and daughters' prophesying (Joel 2:28; Acts 2:17). Believers should first seek the written Word for direction. However, they can encourage each other through prophecy. It is incumbent upon trained and seasoned five-fold prophets to insure that prophecy among the believers maintains the spirit of edification, exhortation and comfort (1Corinthians 14:3).

God still uses the prophet to speak into the earth. Mature prophets are trusted by God to audibly speak His will concerning individuals, groups and nations. The prophetic voice will be crucial during this transitional season in the church as masses of believers will need to be clear regarding the direction and purpose of God.

## Evangelist

When Paul instructed Timothy, he understood that Timothy would soon be on his own (2Timothy 4:6-8). In both letters he wrote to Timothy, his practical tutoring gave his young protégé the tools he needed to succeed. "Fight the good fight of faith" (1Timothy 6:12), "endure hardness as a good soldier" (2Timothy 2:3), and "study to show yourself approved to God" (2Timothy 2:15) are some of the most well-known advice Paul gave to his spiritual son (1Timothy 1:2).

Of all the advice Paul gave Timothy, one in particular was pivotal to him being successful. In 2Timothy 4:5 we read:

*But watch thou in all things, endure afflictions, do the work of an evangelist, make full proof of thy ministry.*

This verse can be summed up in four words – *watch, endure, do* then *make*. It is interesting to note that *'doing the work of an evangelist'* is one of three parts Paul deemed necessary to culminate in *'making full proof of his ministry'*. In other words, the full proof of whatever ministry you or I believe we are called to is determined by our willingness to watch, endure and do the work of an evangelist.

Paul did not explain what an evangelist was. He simply told Timothy to do the work of one. This presupposes that Timothy understood what an evangelist does.

When Jesus ascended, one of the ministry gifts He gave was that of the Evangelist (Ephesians 4:11). In the King James Version of the bible, the word evangelist appears only three times, and in each instance it was translated from the Greek word *euanggelistes*. This word describes a preacher or messenger of good news.

Two other Greek words used in New Testament help us to understand the ministry of an evangelist. *Euaggelizo* means to announce good news or glad tidings. *Euaggelion* refers to the gospel or the good message. Dr. Kevin Connor summarizes that *"the Evangelist is a person with a distinctive ministry, and is a bearer of the message of good news in the saving Gospel of Christ."*[13]

The first work of a five-fold evangelist is internal. Their first work is in and to the church. The spirit of evangelism must never wane in the church. The house church, simple church, organic church or any other kind of church has no basis for existence outside of the message of salvation through Jesus Christ. The Kingdom of God expands as more and more people come to accept the death, burial and victorious resurrection of Jesus Christ.

I believe one of the foremost reasons evangelists are needed is to insure that the redemptive message is maintained in the church. The evangelist must insure that the good news of Jesus Christ is not lost in the teaching of house, simple or organic church methodologies.

The second ministry of the evangelist is external. They are used by God to stir up new territories. Phillip, described as an evangelist (Acts 21:8), preached Christ in Samaria (Acts 8:5-8). His message set the stage for Peter and John to be sent to Samaria by the apostles in Jerusalem. As the New Testament structure evolves in this era, seasoned evangelist may be used by the Lord to stir up new territories.

The evangelist must preach Christ – not church structural methodology. Apostles can follow them, reinforcing the message of Jesus Christ and simultaneously establish structure and order. The Holy Spirit will then identify elders who will be appointed by the apostles to oversee this new territory. This is not hypothetical hyperbole. It is an example of what is possible today through the same Holy Spirit who orchestrated the affairs of the church in the first century.

Pastors

The role of the pastor needs the most revamping of all the ministry gifts. We have been so accustomed to the one pastor – one church model that any other form seems awkward. The role of pastor has been elevated as the preeminent office in the church. The New Testament does not support that model.

The Greek word *poimen* is found in seventeen verses throughout the New Testament. In all but one instance, it is translated as shepherd. Ephesians 4:11 is the only time it is translated as *pastor*. We have seen earlier that *poimen* refers to the manner in which an elder does his work (see chapter 7). Implicit in this is that all pastors are elders. Jesus gave Pastors as one of the five ascension gifts to His church. Some of them are elders, most of them are not. Let me explain.

Paul asked a significant series of questions to the Corinthian church.

*Are all apostles? are all prophets? are all teachers? are all workers of miracles?(1Corinthian 12:29)*

The answer to each question is obviously 'no'. The root Greek word for apostle (*apostolos*) means a sent one. The act of sending is the Greek word *apostello*. In Romans 10:15, we find the same Greek words describing the ministry of an evangelist (*euagelizo*) connected to the Greek word referring to sending (*apostello*). We can assume that Philip was *sent* by the Holy Spirit to Samaria, and we know that an angel of the Lord *sent* him to the Ethiopian eunuch. Yet, Philip is described as an evangelist – not an apostle or elder (Acts 21:8).

Scripture shows us that the Ephesian believers who received the Holy Ghost began to prophesy (Acts 19:6). Paul taught that 'all can prophesy' (1Corinthians 14:31). Philip had four daughters who prophesied (Acts 21:9). Yet, only a few individuals were specifically identified as prophets – Agabus (Acts 11:27-28; 21:10), some of the group who set Barnabas and Saul forth in ministry (Acts 13:1), and Judas and Silas (Acts 15:32). Scripture is clear that although a person may be moved by the Holy Spirit to prophesy, it does not mean the person is to be labeled a prophet.

Paul's instructions to Timothy to "*do the work of an evangelist*" is for all believers. Yet, all believers are not called to the five-fold gift of the Evangelist. Likewise, there are those whose ministry is *pastoral* in nature, but they are not five-fold Pastors or elders.

The biblical structure for the church begins in the house. House churches are identified by the owner, and generally, the ministry of the house owner is pastoral in nature. It is also possible that the house owner simply provides a place of gathering and another member of the group assumes the pastoral role.

The five-fold pastor is also active in a house church, but is also gifted to serve, mentor and assist those who are pastoral. This example can be found in the Old Testament when Moses established rulers over hundreds, fifties and tens (Exodus 18:21-25; Deuteronomy 1:15). Moses selected 'able men' to do this work. He did not select 'elders', even though elders were available (Exodus 3:16; Leviticus 9:1; Numbers 11:16). Likewise, the five-fold Pastor may not necessarily be an elder. What sets them apart from those who are pastoral is their proven gift to serve several pastoral leaders.

The modern day whole church, consisting of several house churches in a city or region will have several 'Pastors' helping to shepherd the local flock. Remember, elders are *governmental* in nature, and the five-fold ministry gifts are *developmental* in nature. It is the collective work of the five-fold ministry that brings maturity. Pastors provide the nurturing spiritual care and personal ministry needed to keep a church healthy.

Teachers
Teachers are needed at all levels of individual and church development. The new believer needs to be taught holiness, sound

doctrine and the Kingdom life. Aspiring ministry leaders need to be taught biblical apologetics. During this season of transition, all believers need to understand how the New Testament structure works. Sound, mature teaching is vital.

> For he taught them as [one] having authority, and not as the scribes. (Matthew 7:29)

> And they were astonished at his doctrine: for he taught them as one that had authority, and not as the scribes.( Mark 1:22)

> Which things also we speak, not in the words which man's wisdom teacheth, but which the Holy Ghost teacheth; comparing spiritual things with spiritual. (1Corithians 2:13)

The five-fold Teacher is one who is gifted to impart biblical truth. Their teaching goes beyond *information* to *impartation*. Information connects with the mind, whereas impartation connects with the spirit. This can span the gambit of topics – from budgets or beliefs to property or prayer, anointed five-fold teachers connect with the spirit of men and women.

Some have erroneously concluded that human teachers are unnecessary. They believe that teaching is done exclusively by the Holy Spirit (1John 2:27). The bible does in fact say that the Holy Spirit will teach us all things (John 14:26), but Godly anointed teachers are crucial to taking apostolic and prophetic foundations and imparting them into the believer's life. We must never forget that the Holy Spirit is the Teacher, and that Jesus Christ is the Great Teacher. Yet, Jesus still appointed Teachers through which the Holy Spirit will work to impart spiritual truth.

We live in a time when people are bombarded with all kinds of beliefs. Even among those claiming to be Christians there is such a hodge-podge of mixed doctrines that it becomes difficult for anyone to know what they believe. Five-fold Teachers must be sound in doctrine. Their inspired instruction should leave no doubts in the heart of those being taught (Acts 6:10).

The church should be ever growing and ever maturing. The gifts of apostle, prophet, evangelist, pastor and teacher together bring the spiritual dimension necessary to bring it to the 'stature of the fullness of Christ'. Maturity eliminates deception brought on by frivolous 'winds of doctrine'. The developmental leadership provided by five-fold ministry gifts insures that 'every joint' or each member of the body supplies their gift which increases the body as a whole.

# No Longer Deacons As Usual     10

Apostles and prophets lay foundations for the church. Elders govern and protect the church. Five-fold ministers equip the saints in order to mature the church. Interwoven throughout all of this activity is the ministry of the deacon.

The deacon is one of the most misunderstood ministries in the church. Depending on the type of church, a deacon can be considered anything from low-grade clergy to a board of directors. In some churches deacons have no authority or esteemed recognition while in others they control everything including the hiring and firing of the pastor.

Much of what we see today regarding deacons reflect our understanding (or possibly misunderstanding) of church structure. It is difficult, if not nearly impossible for deacons to serve accurately within the current church models. The freedom they need to carry out their duties is currently limited to pseudo-sacerdotal functions within a controlled religious environment.

Let's look at the role of the deacon by first looking at the Greek words transliterated in the bible. These will shed light on how we define the word 'deacon'.

The first word *diakonos*, a noun is used thirty–two times in the Greek text. It is translated as *deacon* five times, *servant* seven times and *minister* twenty times. It generally means '*a servant of the people*'. The second Greek noun is *diakonia* which is defined as '*a service or ministry to the people*'. Note the subtle difference. The first Greek word *diakonos* describes a servant '*of*' the people, whereas this second word describes a servant '*to*' the people. In the King James Version of the bible, the second word *diakonia* is used thirty-four times. Sixteen times it is translated as *ministry*, six times as *ministration*, three times as *ministering*, two times as service, two times as *administration*, one time each as *relief, office, do service and to minister*.

The second Greek word is closely aligned with a Greek verb, *diakoneo* which means '*to wait upon or serve the people*'. It is *the act of serving*. This word is used thirty-seven times in Greek text. What makes this verb significant is that it is used both in an *unofficial sense* delineating the work of basic household servants, and describes the many ways people minister and serve one another. It is also used in an *official sense* relating specifically to those appointed to the *office of a deacon*.

Jesus Christ gives us the greatest example of what a deacon should be. He had the spirit of a servant. He came to serve.

> But Jesus called them unto him, and said, Ye know that the princes of the Gentiles exercise dominion over them, and they that are great exercise authority upon them. But it shall not be so among you: but whosoever will be great among you, let him be your minister [diakonos]; And whosoever will be chief among you, let him be your servant[14]: Even as the Son of man came not to be ministered [diakoneo] unto, but to minister [diakoneo], and to give his life a ransom for many. (Matthew 20:25-28)

Jesus taught that every member of the Body of Christ should be a servant. No one is exempt from walking in the spirit of a deacon. This first includes every elder and ascension gift. It includes every blood-washed believer. In our hierarchal crazed church world, some church 'leaders' do not feel they are fulfilled without an entourage of armor bearers, water bringers, briefcase carriers and vehicle drivers. This is a complete aberration of the teachings of Jesus. All believers should seek to serve one another (Matthew 23:11; Galatians 5:13).

What sets the deacon apart from other believers is the use of the word 'office'. Twice Paul mentioned the 'office of a deacon'. The word 'office' is used eight times in the King James Version of the New Testament.

Like many words translated into English, the word 'office' is translated from several Greek words. The reader needs to be clear which 'office' is being used in each text. Generally speaking, the word office implies an *official capacity*. Three times the word 'office' is used in relation to priest (Luke 1:8-9; Hebrews 7:5). The Greek noun *hierateia* and the Greek verb *hierateuo* are used. The noun describes the official-ness of the priests, whereas the verb speaks to the execution of what they do.

In another text, Paul magnified his apostolic office (Romans 11:13). It is remarkable that the Greek word he used for office is *diakonia*, which is that of being a minister or servant to the people. This should send a clear signal to all contemporary apostles. You are called by the Lord to serve.

Later when Paul taught about the various gifts in the Body of Christ, he stated that all members do not have the same office (Romans 12:4-13). Here the Greek word '*praxis*' is used. This word describes a function. In other words, Paul states that the members of the Body of Christ do not serve in the same capacity, but they all bear the responsibility to minister to one another. In first Timothy 3:1 Paul mentions those who desire the 'office of a bishop'. Here the Greek word *episkope* is used. As we have learned before, *episkope* is one of three words used to describe an elder – specifically his work.

Finally, we come to the '*office of a deacon*'. Twice this phrase is used in the third chapter of first Timothy (verses 10 and 13). In both cases the Greek word *diakaneo* is used. It is the same word used as one who serves and ministers to the people. It is the same word Paul used to describe his apostolic office. Here, with the deacon, we find one appointed to serve and minister to the people in an official capacity.

Most theologians hold that deacons are appointed to their office. That appointment does not circumvent the need for the deacon to be fully qualified to hold the office. Thus we see in first Timothy chapter three, qualifications that nearly equal that of an elder. This reveals that deacons cannot be weak or shallow in their faith. They cannot have dysfunctional families or marriages, or else they would be disqualified from serving in this official capacity. Both the elder and the deacon '*must first be proved*', but this requirement is specifically listed for the deacons (1Timothy 3:10). The deacon is a valuable ministry in the church and needs to be fully understood.

## THE NATURE OF THE DEACON

Apostles and prophets are *foundational*. Apostles and Elders are *governmental*. Ascension gifts are *developmental*. Deacons are *servant-al*. Servant-al is a word I devised to express the nature of the work of the deacon. Serving is the primary function and nature of their work in the church.

Paul often used the analogy of the human body to describe the Body of Christ (1Corinthians 12:15-24). Please allow me to do the same in order to illustrate the ministry of the deacon.

Within your body is a heart, brain, muscles, bones, etc. Each of these vital organs require blood to survive (Leviticus 17:11-14; Deuteronomy 12:23). The only way blood can get to these organs is through a system of blood vessels. The blood vessels are like the ministry of the deacon. The blood vessels are not the blood (which travels through them), or the brain (which provides direction), the heart (that pumps the blood), the muscles (the strength of the body) or bones (the structure of the body). Yet, the blood vessels serve to provide access for the blood to get to each of these organs.

Likewise, the deacons are not the elders, apostles or the other ascension gifts per se, but they serve to provide access for life giving resources to flow throughout the local church. That is why the ministry of the deacon is *servant-al*.

If blood vessels become clogged or closed, they can weaken or even kill the body. If the deacons fail to carry life giving resources throughout the local church, that church will be weak at best, but could potentially die.

> And in those days, when the number of the disciples was multiplied, there arose a murmuring of the Grecians against the Hebrews, because their widows were neglected in the daily ministration. Then the twelve called the multitude of the disciples unto them, and said, It is not reason that we should leave the word of God, and serve tables. Wherefore, brethren, look ye out among you seven men of honest report, full of the Holy Ghost and wisdom, whom we may appoint over this business. But we will give ourselves continually to prayer, and to the ministry of the word. And the saying pleased the whole multitude: and they chose Stephen, a man full of faith and of the Holy Ghost, and Philip, and Prochorus, and Nicanor, and Timon, and Parmenas, and Nicolas a proselyte of Antioch: Whom they set before the apostles: and when they had prayed, they laid their hands on them. And the word of God increased; and the number of the disciples multiplied in Jerusalem greatly; and a great company of the priests were obedient to the faith. (Acts 6:1-7)

There two things we must understand and glean from this passage. First, no where in this text were the seven men selected and appointed specifically called deacons. Second, historically none of the seven men continued in the ministry of 'waiting on tables' at the behest of the apostles. But their appointment does shed light on the effect an *appointed servant* can have on the church.

These seven men were chosen as a result of a specific need in the church at that time. The Greek widows were being neglected in the daily ministry of resources. The Apostles clearly empathized with the need and took responsibility in resolving it. But in doing so, they felt their personal time would be best spent by remaining *'continually in prayer, and in ministry of the word'* (Acts 6:4). Thus, their appointment was two-fold – to meet the needs of the Grecian widows without encumbering the work of the Apostles. This all occurred around 33 A.D., the same year of the great day of Pentecost.

## THIRTY YEAR EVOLUTION OF THE DEACON

Again, note that the seven men in Acts 6 were not labeled as deacons, but they clearly were enlisted for a specific service. But if it is questionable that this occurrence was the advent of the deacon, we must ask when did 'deacons' become a formalized ministry in the church? Surprisingly, the answer is unknown. Twenty-eight years after the 'Grecian widow' incident (A.D. 61) Paul wrote the church at Philippi and addressed them as follows:

> *Paul and Timotheus, the servants of Jesus Christ, to all the saints in Christ Jesus which are at Philippi, <u>with the bishops[15] and deacons</u>: (Philippians 1:1)*

Without describing who they were, Paul addressed the elders *and deacons* of Philippi. Somewhere in the twenty-eight years following Pentecost the role of deacons evolved, presumably to work with local elders to meet needs that arose in the church. The fact that Philippi appeared to have active deacons, does not imply that other churches did not employ them also. This was just the first formal recognition of them.

The seriousness of their role became more apparent two years later (A.D. 63) when Paul instructed Timothy regarding the qualifications for deacons (1Timothy 3:8-13). So about thirty years after Pentecost the deacon was an apparent active ministry in the New Testament Church.

No where in scripture are the specific functions of a deacon found, except in the implicit title they carry meaning *'to serve'*. This is why various contemporary church systems have created their own 'job description' for the deacon. Without specific functions from scripture, we must rely on the implicit meaning of the Greek words associated with deacons – *diakonos, diakonia and diakoneo*. None of them imply being a *'board of director'* type role. They always serve under the authority of the local elders.

## Deacons Today

Finally, the ministry of deacons seems to exist on an *'as needed'* basis. In other words, all members of the local assembly can serve each other for the benefit of the church. However, if there are specific needs that would impede the work of the elders, or that require more attention than the local members can handle, then deacons should be appointed. As the New Testament model of the church evolves, there is no doubt that the role of the deacon will be vital.

Contemporary deacons can insure that local and regional church resources are used equitably. They can assist in meeting the welfare needs of members of the local or regional church (i.e. emergency food, clothing and shelter). Wherever needs are unmet in the church, the deacons are the divine servants established in the Word of God to handle them with biblical results.

*And the word of God increased; and the number of the disciples multiplied in Jerusalem greatly; and a great company of the priests were obedient to the faith. (Acts 6:7)*

# The Values of New Testament Church    11

Throughout the New Testament we discover the values embraced by the first century believers expressed in phrases like "...*the believers were together and had all things in common*" (Acts 2:44) or, "...*the multitude of them that believed were of one heart and of one soul: neither said any of them that ought of the things which he possessed was his own; but they had all things common*" (Acts 4:32). It is reflected in "...*the God of patience and consolation grant you to be likeminded one toward another according to Christ Jesus: That ye may with one mind and one mouth glorify God, even the Father of our Lord Jesus Christ. Wherefore receive ye one another, as Christ also received us to the glory of God* (Romans 15:5-7). Values help us to understand each others motives and increase our ability to walk as one.

## VALUES PRECEDE DOCTRINE

The values of the first century church preceded the myriad of doctrines we see today. The values are the normative practices gleaned from the first century church during a time when the only doctrine was the Doctrines of Christ (Hebrews 6:1) as taught by the Apostles (Acts 2:42), and lived out through personal doctrine (1Corinthian 14:26).

Values are usually unwritten. They are usually practiced with no conscious forethought. Nearly every action is linked to a value. Decisions are based on values. Most people have no clue what the values are in the Kingdom of God or the New Testament Church. They are the values of the King – Jesus Christ. In this season of reformation, members in the New Testament church need to be acutely aware of the values of the Kingdom of God and how they are expressed in the earth through the church.

The New Testament reveals five values that created the basis for doctrine in the first century church. These values are imperative to be a normal citizen in the Kingdom. Again, I want to emphasize that these are not 'doctrines' but values that undergird all doctrines that exist. The five values are:

1.  The Lordship of Jesus Christ

2.  The Priesthood of every believer

3.  The Holy Spirit

4.  Growth through covenant relationships

5.  No one among us lacks

## VALUE 1: THE LORDSHIP OF JESUS CHRIST

Jesus is Lord! Every knee shall bow, every tongue must confess the Lordship of Jesus Christ (Philippians 2:11). Salvation is impossible without first acknowledging that Jesus is Lord (Romans 9:9). The Holy Spirit empowers you to say, "Jesus is Lord" (1 Corinthians 12:3). If we miss, misunderstand or neglect this first and primary value, then everything else we do is null and void. There is no reason to discuss any other value if we overlook this first and primary value – the Lordship of Jesus Christ.

In the first century, everything the believers did rose and fell on this one value – the Lordship of Jesus Christ. If they gathered, they gathered around Jesus Christ (Matthew 18:20; Colossians 3:17). If they preached, it was all about Jesus Christ (Acts 17:3; 1Corinthians 15:3-4; 2Corinthians 4:5). If they taught, they taught about Jesus (Acts 5:42). Like Paul, they knew their very existence centered around the Lordship of Jesus Christ (Colossians 1:27; Galatians 2:20).

Believers in the first century understood a 'lord' to be *the sole owner*. The first century church understood that Jesus Christ was not one of many options (Deuteronomy 6:4; Mark 12:29; Galatians 3:20). They did not view Him as just one answer among a series of multiple choices (Acts 4:12; 1Timothy 2:5-6). He is not the choice of A – B – C – D or None of the above. First century believers understood that once you made Jesus Christ an option, you have essentially eliminated Him as Lord in your life.

Recently we had a question and answer period during an evening gathering. I had been teaching for several weeks regarding the Lordship of Jesus Christ. One the first questions was "What exactly is the Lordship of Jesus Christ?" Even though I had been teaching it for several weeks, for a brief moment I had to think about my answer.

The Holy Spirit prompted me to say "When we make Jesus Christ Lord, we willfully give up all of our right to opinions." We are totally bought with a price, and we no longer have a right to our way of doing things (1Corinthians 6:19-20).

As Americans, we take pride in our rights. We have a right to this – we have a right to that. We defend our right to free speech – to bear arms – to worship as we please. But when we give our lives to Jesus Christ, our rights immediately disappear as we totally submit to Him. The values of His Kingdom supersede the rights we embrace in our constitution.

Yes, our American Constitution gives us the right to free speech. But the Word of God says "... when they shall lead you, and deliver you up, take no thought beforehand what ye shall speak, neither do ye premeditate: but whatsoever shall be given you in that hour, that speak ye: for it is not ye that speak, but the Holy Ghost" (Mark 13:11). Yes, we can bear arms to defend ourselves, but what do you do with Matthew 5:39.[16] It is a blessing to live in a country where we can worship where we please. Jesus was not concerned with our location of religious activity but rather he was concerned with our heart (John 4:21-24). Everything we do must be built on the one basic foundational truth – that Jesus Christ Is Lord!

## VALUE 2: THE PRIESTHOOD OF THE BELIEVER

One of the teachings espoused by Martin Luther in the sixteenth century reformation was the priesthood of the believer. He taught that each of us can approach the Father, in Jesus' Name, without the assistance of a human intermediary. He taught that we are all priest and can approach the Lord on our own (Hebrews 4:16; 1Peter 2:9).

The New Testament Church is a permissional culture and the priesthood of the believer is a key foundation of that culture.

> *And the veil of the temple was rent in twain from the top to the bottom (Mark 15:38).*

> *Having therefore, brethren, boldness to enter into the holiest by the blood of Jesus, By a new and living way, which he hath consecrated for us, through the veil, that is to say, his flesh (Hebrews 10:19-20).*

When Jesus was crucified, the veil that separated the inner court from the Holy of Holies was torn from TOP to BOTTOM. It was the proof that through the blood of Jesus Christ, God has given us direct access to Him. The implication of the veil being torn from top to bottom is that access came from heaven to earth – from God to man. Had it been torn from bottom to top it would imply a forced attempt of man towards God. Because God opened the access, we can now approach the Throne of Grace boldly to find grace to help in the time of need. This access is available to every believer (Hebrews 4:16).

## WHICH KIND OF PRIEST ARE YOU?

> *And take thou unto thee Aaron thy brother, and his sons with him, from among the children of Israel, <u>that he may minister unto me in the priest's office</u>, even Aaron, Nadab and Abihu, Eleazar and Ithamar, Aaron's sons (Exodus 28:1).*

> *Yet they shall be ministers in my sanctuary, having charge at the gates of the house, and ministering to the house: they shall slay the burnt offering and the sacrifice for the people, and they shall stand before them to minister unto them (Ezekiel 44:11).*

*But I will make them keepers of the charge of the house, for all the service thereof, and for all that shall be done therein (Ezekiel 44:14).*

*As they ministered to the Lord, and fasted, the Holy Ghost said, Separate me Barnabas and Saul for the work whereunto I have called them (Acts 13:2).*

There are two categories of priest described in scripture. There are those *who minister to the house,* and those *who minister to the Lord.* From the onset, we see in Exodus 28:1 that God intended for the priest to minister to Him. In Ezekiel 44:11 we find a group of priests that only ministered to the house. They are those who had compromised their relationship with the Lord. They had allowed sin to flourish in the temple. It is interesting that God did not disqualify them from being a priest; He simply stopped them from ministering to Him. Here we find that God's value is not based on what we do 'in the church', but rather He values our ministry to Him (Matthew 7:21-23).

Our carnal nature enjoys the feeling of receiving human accolades. Seeking the applause of flesh is proof that you are only ministering to the house. We must seek to please the Lord alone (1 Corinthians 10:31; Revelation 4:11).

*But ye are a chosen generation, a royal priesthood, an holy nation, a peculiar people; that ye should shew forth the praises of him who hath called you out of darkness into his marvellous light (1 Peter 2:9)*

To be a priest unto the Lord is to minister TO Him and not FOR Him. Others may possibly witness or benefit from our ministry to Him, but our sole motive should be to please Him and Him alone.

When Saul and Barnabas were selected by the Holy Ghost for a work, five men were 'ministering to the Lord' when the Holy Spirit revealed their assignment (Acts 13:2). Your gifts and your calling *are birthed from ministering to the Lord*, not from looking for something to do to impress others.

> *And hath made us kings and priests unto God and his Father; to him be glory and dominion for ever and ever. Amen. (Revelation 1:6)*

> *And hast made us unto our God kings and priests: and we shall reign on the earth. (Revelation 5:10)*

The priesthood of the believer must be understood in functional terms rather than in titles. God sees us as kings and priest. It is not important that we are called priests, it is only important that we do what the priests are called to do.

The first thing we must recognize is our equality in Jesus Christ. In Christ, we are all spiritually equal. You are a priest in the sight of God. I am a priest in the sight of God. There is only one high priest among us – Jesus Christ (Hebrews 3:1; 4:14; 6:20). It is imperative that I submit to the work of Christ in you as much as you submit to the work of Christ in me (Galatians 3:28; Ephesians 5;21; Philippians 2:3). We must recognize that the primary work of Christ in us is not the manifestation of a particular gift, but rather the process of conforming us to His image (Romans 8:29; Galatians 4:19).

Being a priest is not to be a 'god unto ourselves' (Romans 10:3). It is when we acknowledge Christ in each other. It is allowing each person to express Christ as He is revealed within them. It is recognizing the significance Christ produces in each person. More importantly, it is submitting to that expression of Christ in our brothers and sisters.

*And he ordained twelve, <u>that they should be with him</u>, and that he might send them forth to preach, (Mark 3:14 KJV)*

Jesus' first ordination of His disciples was simply that they be with Him. The greatest thing you can do as a believer is to sit at the feet of Jesus. As priests, our gifts and callings are subject to His command for His glory. This brings us to the third value.

## VALUE 3: THE HOLY SPIRIT

Jesus is Lord over his Church. The Holy Spirit is the sole managing agent of His church in the earth. It is not elders or five-fold gifts. The third value that believers in the first century embraced was the work of the Holy Spirit in their daily lives. No decision was made or action taken if they were not directed by the Holy Spirit.

*And when they had prayed, the place was shaken where they were assembled together; and they were all filled with the Holy Ghost, and they spake the word of God with boldness. (Acts 4:31)*

Being filled with the Holy Spirit was normative for first century believers. There was no doctrine of pneumatology. There was no study of glossalia. It was simply the normal practice to be filled, empowered and led by the Holy Ghost. The filling of the Holy Ghost produced the boldness they had to speak the Word of God.

*As they ministered to the Lord, and fasted, the Holy Ghost said, Separate me Barnabas and Saul for the work whereunto I have called them. (Acts 13:2)*

The Holy Ghost set individuals into ministry. The first century church understood that those who served the body of Christ required the sanctioning of the Holy Ghost.

*So they, being sent forth by the Holy Ghost, departed unto Seleucia; and from thence they sailed to Cyprus. (Acts 13:4)*

*Now when they had gone throughout Phrygia and the region of Galatia, and were forbidden of the Holy Ghost to preach the word in Asia, (Acts 16:6)*

The Holy Ghost determined where the believers ministered. Another example is Phillip the evangelist. He was directed by the Spirit to the Ethiopian eunuch. He preached Jesus Christ to him, baptized him, then in an instant the Spirit took Phillip away (Acts 8:29-39).

*Take heed therefore unto yourselves, and to all the flock, over the which the Holy Ghost hath made you overseers, to feed the church of God, which he hath purchased with his own blood. (Acts 20:28)*

Even though the apostles ordained elders, the Holy Ghost made them overseers. Those who released others into ministry thoroughly understood that it was the leading of the Holy Ghost (Acts 13:3-4).

*Which things also we speak, not in the words which man's wisdom teacheth, but which the Holy Ghost teacheth; comparing spiritual things with spiritual. (1Corinthian 2:13)*

The Holy Ghost was considered the teacher of the believers. He could effectively compare spiritual things with spiritual. Jesus had promised that the Holy Spirit would lead them into all truth and teach them all things. Therefore the first century believer only spoke what the Holy Spirit taught them (John 14:26; 16:13)

> But Peter said, Ananias, why hath Satan filled thine heart to lie to the Holy Ghost, and to keep back part of the price of the land? (Acts 5:3)

The apostles knew that people lied against Holy Ghost – not them. The believers learned that without the direction of the Holy Ghost, their efforts were fruitless. Jesus had taught that blasphemy against the Holy Ghost was deadly, and Apostle Paul urged the believers not to grieve Him (Matthew 12:31; Ephesians 4:30).

> Now the God of hope fill you with all joy and peace in believing, that ye may abound in hope, through the power of the Holy Ghost. (Romans 15:13)

The only reason any ministry, spiritual or grace gift should ever be exercised, is to build up another believer or group of believers so that their gifts can be used to build up other believers

> What? know ye not that your body is the temple of the Holy Ghost [which is] in you, which ye have of God, and ye are not your own? (1Corinthians 6:19)

## THE GIFTS OF THE HOLY SPIRIT

The institutional church has put the cart ahead of the horse when it comes to spiritual gifts. Everybody wants to be something – an apostle, prophet, or evangelist, etc. People clamor for ordination and public recognition.

I was once approached by a man who wanted me to ordain him as an elder – so that he could be one. He had no concept that even with our institutional mindset, ordination is a confirmation of work already done. In his thinking, he felt that once he was ordained, he would magically become an elder.

I attempt to remain close to whatever the Lord is doing in the earth. I fully embraced the prophetic and apostolic reformation of the last fifteen years. As the prophetic movement progressed, we eagerly sought out 'prophetic conferences' and events. On several occasions we hosted workshops where we received 'prophetic impartations'. For a time our congregation seemed to be blessed by what we were learning. It didn't take long for problems to show up. In my book PROPHETIC JUDGMENT, I addressed some of the dysfunction that started emerging.[17]

In a short period of time, we found ourselves surrounded by dozens of 'prophetically activated' believers. Because of the traditional church structure, all of these prophetically activated believers had very little outlet to express themselves. Only a limited number of people could be released to minister during worship services. I became inundated with individuals claiming that God had called them to be prophets. Some of these people were hardly believers, but expected me to 'ordain' them as prophets.

Other churches in the area had also activated their members in the prophetic ministry. So occasionally we would fellowship with them and their prophetic teams would minister to our members. Later, we would visit their church and our prophetic team would minister to them. This too seemed so inadequate and pointless. During one message I described what we were doing as being prophetically incestuous.

As I sought the Lord, He reminded me of an instruction He had given me several years ago to "Provide a viable outlet for all ministry gifts". Although I didn't immediately connect this with the New Testament Church structure, I did begin to see that only in small groups could this be possible. My bureaucratic nature clicked in and I sought ways to make this happen. I am thankful that the Holy Spirit arrested my fleshly ideas before I went too far.

The church as seen in the New Testament is the only catalyst by which EVERY ministry, spiritual and grace gift can function as the Lord intended. In traditional church settings, gifts are generally exhibited through individuals who are *ministering to the house at best, and spiritual exhibitionist as its worst.* That is why so many were claiming to be called as prophets. They saw an opportunity to be in the forefront – to be in the limelight and have a *ministry* of their own. Paul addressed this issue to the Corinthian church.

> *Now concerning spiritual gifts, brethren, I would not have you ignorant. Ye know that ye were Gentiles, carried away unto these dumb idols, even as ye were led. (1Corithians 12:1-2)*

I know that the word 'dumb' in the above passage is translated as mute, but I also think it is somewhat comical that the King James Version calls spiritual gifts 'dumb' idols, when in fact chasing after gifts as a validation of spirituality is dumb!

In the church first century church, the close relationships created an atmosphere of accountability. All gifts were held accountable to each other. It was hard to give an off-the-wall prophesy in a setting where it can be judged. In the house church, gifts are used by the Holy Spirit to build the believers, not promote the one exercising the gift. This brings us to an important point.

The only reason any ministry, spiritual or grace gift should ever be exercised, is to build up another believer or group of believers so that their gifts can be used to build up other believers.

The moment we begin to seek any form of notoriety for the use of any gift, we have crossed the line where Jesus is no longer Lord, our priesthood (ministry to the Lord) is tainted and the gift itself is reduced to a toy.

## VALUE 4: GROWTH THROUGH COVENANT RELATIONSHIPS

*...there should be no schism in the body; but that the members should have the same care one for another. And whether one member suffer, all the members suffer with it; or one member be honoured, all the members rejoice with it. Now ye are the body of Christ, and members in particular (1Corinthians 12:25-27)*

My friend Donald R. Todd taught me a unique biblical truth. It appears the *believers were added* to the church, then they were *added to the Lord*, and finally the *disciples and churches were multiplied.*

In the early days immediately following Pentecost, there was much excitement regarding the Gospel. Jesus did not leave a 'church start-up manual' for the thousands who had received the Gospel message. The first group of believers simply connected with the original one hundred and twenty from the upper room. The bible says the three thousand souls were *added to them.*

*Then they that gladly received his word were baptized: and the same day there were <u>added unto them</u> about three thousand souls (Acts 2:41).*

*Praising God, and having favour with all the people. And the Lord*
*added to the church daily such as should be saved (Acts 2:47).*

It became apparent that these believers began fellowshipping intensely. They had all things in common, and continued daily in the temple and from house to house. These relationships became recognized as '*the church*' to which souls were *added* daily.

*And believers were the more added to the Lord, multitudes both of men*
*and women (Acts 5:14).*

*For [Barnabas] was a good man, and full of the Holy Ghost and of faith:*
*and much people was added unto the Lord (Acts 11:24).*

The next two groups were added to the Lord. Immediately following the death of Ananias and Sapphira people feared the Lord. The apostles refused to take the glory for what God was doing. The people did not join themselves to the apostles, but directly to the Lord. As a result of the persecution against the new believers, Barnabas went to Antioch to exhort and encourage the saints. Again scripture says many people were added to the Lord.

Let's review the progression. On the Day of Pentecost, the people were stirred by the manifested presence of the Holy Ghost in the apostles and one hundred and twenty believers from the upper room. They wanted to receive this power, and wanted to connect with these newly filled believers. So they were added to '*them*' – the apostles and the one hundred twenty (Acts 2:41). They became a collective group identified as the church. Daily people were added to the church.

The first value the apostles taught was the Lordship of Jesus Christ (Acts 5:42). The church was growing, but the apostles made sure that the focus remained Jesus Christ alone. Peter clearly did not take credit for the deaths of Ananias and Sapphira. The lies they told were to the Holy Ghost and not to him (Acts 5:3). Thus, the focus always remained on Jesus Christ. The result is that believers were added to the Lord (Acts 5:14).

Finally, even under intense persecution, the apostles could have emerged as heroic martyrs. Instead, they counted themselves honored to suffer for the Name of the Lord. Barnabas did not preach an "I've been through the fire" message, instead he preached Jesus and more people were added to the Lord.

*And the word of God increased; and the number of the disciples multiplied in Jerusalem greatly; and a great company of the priests were obedient to the faith (Acts 6:7).*

*Then had the churches rest throughout all Judaea and Galilee and Samaria, and were edified; and walking in the fear of the Lord, and in the comfort of the Holy Ghost, were multiplied (Acts 9:31).*

Later fruit of covenant relationships became apparent. Obviously the believers began discipling one another (from house to house I may add). They were beginning to do what Jesus had commanded (Matthew 28:19). The results were phenomenal. Growth shifted from adding to multiplying.

The gathering from house to house was key in birthing the Church. What they did in those houses was equally as important. They broke bread, shared meals and supported one another. They also exhorted, encouraged and taught one another. House churches did not appear to split, but rather to multiply. Implicit in the supernatural growth was a practice to leave one house church for the purpose of starting a new house church. There is no other explanation for their exponential growth.

Growth, spiritual and numerical, is a value we must embrace. Individuals must grow in grace and in the knowledge of Jesus Christ (2 Peter 3:18). Equally, believers must grow in covenant relationship with each other. The *'rejoice with those who rejoice and cry with those who cry'* must be coupled with *'having all things in common'* (Acts 2:44; 4:32; 1Corinthians 12:26).

## VALUE 5: NO ONE AMONG US SHALL LACK

I will lay my possessions down for the benefit of other believers. My goal is more than meeting their needs in the time of crisis. I want to insure that they do not lack so that they can function in the body more effectively

*And all that believed were together, and had all things common; And sold their possessions and goods, and parted them to all men, as every man had need. (Acts 2:44-45)*

*And the multitude of them that believed were of one heart and of one soul: neither said any of them that ought of the things which he possessed was his own; but they had all things common. And with great power gave the apostles witness of the resurrection of the Lord Jesus: and great grace was upon them all. Neither was there any among them that lacked: for as many as were possessors of lands or houses sold them, and brought the prices of the things that were sold, And laid them down at the apostles' feet: and distribution was made unto every man according as he had need. And Joses, who by the apostles was surnamed Barnabas, (which is, being interpreted, The son of consolation,) a Levite, and of the country of Cyprus, having land, sold it, and brought the money, and laid it at the apostles' feet. (Acts 4:32-37)*

I am totally amazed at the spirit the believers had in the first century church. They had all things in common. They sold their goods for the benefit of others. They did not consider what they possessed as their own. No one lacked. They practiced *common-ism* not communism. Their hearts were for one another.

In this me-my society we live in, everybody looks out for number one – even in ministry. The early church sold their goods and laid them at the apostle's feet. Today this practice has been grossly distorted. I have watched well-known preachers as thousands of dollars was laid on the altar. Absolutely no needs were met, unless you consider their Bentleys, personal jets and designer suits as needs. I think you get my point.

What is the purpose of the value of *'no one lacking among us'*? Is it just to insure that everyone's personal bills are paid? Is it an exercise in social welfare? These things may happen, but in reality they are not the driving force behind this value.

Do you remember the third value regarding the Holy Spirit? Do you remember the why we exercise the gifts He entrusts to us?

**The only reason any ministry, spiritual or grace gift should ever be exercised, is to build up another believer or group of believers so that their gifts can be used to build up other believers.**

The principle behind *'no one lacking'* is the same. I will lay my possessions down for the benefit of other believers. My goal is more than meeting their needs in the time of crisis. I want to insure that they do not lack so that they can function in the body more effectively.

*No one lacking* is not an empty promise to pay bills, provide food or make believers wealthy, but rather a practice geared to make every believer productive.

## THE EFFECT OF NO ONE LACKING IN THE WORLD

The world is looking for answers. There is global financial distress in nearly every country on earth. Global economists grope at conflicting ideas in humanistic attempts to avoid massive worldwide recession. I believe the only answer is the Church (Ephesians 3:10).

In the church, many have succumbed to the ups and downs of the world economy. They grope after money making schemes and embrace unbiblical and unethical practices. The world sees the church as no different from any other entity in the earth.

The world systems should recognize a difference emanating from the church. We preach our messages that too often fall on spiritually deaf ears. When people see a difference, they will at minimum investigate the matter. The world should find a church of self-sufficient people with purpose, who exhibit the supernatural ability to meet each others needs. They should find a people wherein public welfare is shunned and avoided. They should find a unique body of covenant believers wherein no one among them lacks.

Some reading this may think that I am being a bit idealistic. Everything I believe is rooted in the Word of God, not utopian fantasy. If there were ever a time when a people existed of which no one among them lacked, then I believe such a people can exist today. (Deuteronomy 15:4; 29:5; Acts 4:34)

> *And I will raise me up a faithful priest, that shall do according to that which is in mine heart and in my mind: and I will build him a sure house; and he shall walk before mine anointed for ever. And it shall come to pass, that every one that is left in thine house shall come and crouch to him for a piece of silver and a morsel of bread, and shall say, Put me, I pray thee, into one of the priests' offices, that I may eat a piece of bread. (1Samuel 2:35-36)*

A prophet was sent to Eli to warn and rebuke him for his lackadaisical handling of his sinful sons. The final portion of this prophecy reveals great truth for the church today. The prophet first declared God would raise up a faithful obedient priest of whom God would build a sure house. This faithful priest of course is Jesus Christ, our great High Priest. The sure house is His church (1Timothy 3:15; Hebrews 3:1-6).

The second declaration the prophet made to Eli was that God's faithful priest [Jesus Christ], *'shall walk before [God's] anointed for ever'*. Who are these anointed? They are the blood washed saints of God. Jesus is before us in all things. Jesus Christ is the firstborn among many brethren (Romans 8:29; Hebrews 12:23).

Then the prophet shifted back to the nature of Eli's household declaring that everyone in it would come to the faithful Priest. Notice particularly what their request will be – *"to be put in one of the priests' offices so they could get silver and bread"*. What does this mean?

Religious systems (Eli's house), and world systems (false kingdoms) will collapse. Those who continue in sin and who trust the world systems will one day bow at the feet of Jesus (The Faithful Priest) declaring His Lordship (Philippians 2:11). Also notice that what they needed to survive (silver and bread) came through being in one of the priests' offices.

Do you recall the second value in the Kingdom – the priesthood of all believers? Here is a prophetic example of the impact the Body of Christ should have on world systems. If we function God's way, others will be drawn to Jesus Christ and desire what we have in Him. Silver and bread are not heavenly needs, but rather earthly needs. Those in need were seeking survival goods that they saw in the 'sure house' – the church.

In the New Testament, unbelievers came asking 'What must I do...?" (Acts 2:37; 16:30). When unbelievers see the tangible evidence of the Kingdom, they will want what they see. People followed Jesus because of the miracles (John 2:23). Paul ministered with tangible evidence (1Corinthians 2:4). When contemporary Christians walk in tangible evidence of the Kingdom (Matthew 12:28), lifting up Jesus Christ (John 12:32), then the world will come asking, "What must I do...?" and will desire to be put into one of the priests' office (1Peter 2:9).

Jesus is Lord. Every believer is a priest. The Holy Spirit is directing the Lord's Church. The believers locally and globally are growing through covenant relationships, and no one among us lacks anything needed for life and ministry. These are the values of the New Testament Church.

# No Longer Giving As Usual 12

Whenever there is a change in structure it usually creates a change in all subsequent processes. The structural reformation of the New Testament Church will clearly change the process of handling money.

The local church is a three-fold cord consisting of the house church, the whole church and the temple. The primary gathering of believers begins in the house. Each house church gathering is as much a church as any steepled building you see in your community. The whole church exists to support the house church. The brick and mortar 'temple' is a training and resource center. It is a place of prayer, learning and commerce.

Each house church is autonomous but spiritually connected to every other house church in its city or region. The members of an accurately functioning house church will be in proper relationship with local elders and deacons who establish and implement the guidelines for handling money. Because the house church is autonomous, financial giving should remain with that gathering of believers, to be used within the guidelines established by local elders.

Donations made during whole church gatherings should be voluntary contributions from both the house churches, and individuals. The 'temple' should serve as a place to receive donations which are ear marked for specific purposes. This shift in the flow of resources reflects a significant change to how the church receives and distributes its resources.

## THE IMPACT OF MARTIN LUTHER'S 95 THESIS

Most people are familiar with the birth of the Protestant Reformation when Martin Luther nailed his ninety-five thesis on the door of the Castle Church in Wittenberg. If asked, most would readily speak of Luther's teaching regarding salvation by grace through faith in Jesus Christ alone (Ephesians 2:8), which in fact is one truth he promulgated. However, very few will mention his twenty-eighth point within the thesis:

> It is certain that when the penny jingles into the money-box, gain and avarice can be increased, but the result of the intercession of the Church is in the power of God alone.

Luther wrote the above in objection to a statement purportedly made by Johann Tetzel who popularized the selling of indulgences in order to raise money for construction work being done on Saint Peters Cathedral. Tetzel was in fact selling salvation for the church's building project. Supposedly, his actual statement was, "*As soon as a coin in the coffer rings / the soul from purgatory springs.*" This angered Martin Luther and prompted him to write his now famous ninety-five thesis.

Although Luther did not totally refute the Pope's authority to grant pardons for penance imposed by the Church, he did however make it clear that preachers who claimed the indulgences absolved buyers from all punishments were wrong. The church literally was selling 'forgiveness' to build their personal wealth and their cathedrals.

By exposing the people to the truth of God's word, Luther unwittingly created a *theological* and *financial* reformation. Theologically, he biblically proved the Pope did not have the right to grant pardons in God's behalf. He preached the truth that salvation is by grace through faith in Christ Jesus.[18] This truth simultaneously eliminated the need to purchase indulgences, thus drastically affecting the financial coffers of the church of that day. In fact, Luther challenged the Pope, (who was very wealthy) to spend his own money to build Saint Peter's church.[19]

## THE BIG QUESTION TODAY

The question must be asked, "If there had been no financial ramifications to Luther's 95 Thesis, would the reformation have had the same impact?" I am sure some would have disputed his theological stance, but when you read his entire work, it is clear that the financial impact had the greatest effect. The 'money' issue is still the most common question I hear today in reference to the church structure in the New Testament.

Throughout this book we have discussed the structural change of the New Testament Church. Since beginning my personal studies on this subject, I have often shared my revelations with a variety of church leaders. One question I often hear is, "How is money handled in this New Testament Church structure you propose?" Many of these leaders receive salaries or some other compensation from their church. Money is often the make or break factor for some church leaders.

Churches do not sell indulgences today, but similar tactics are used. Prayer cloths, anointed water, special anointing oil and even a personal prophetic word are the modern day indulgences being sold to the innocent. The flow of money has become so critical that in some cases it is hard to distinguish if Christian meetings are for spiritual edification or fundraising.

The majority of money received in churches is spent on mortgages, salaries, and the upkeep and expansion of existing church facilities. I recently read one statistic that stated that only about two cents of every dollar given goes to overseas missions. This pattern of spending drains the life out of many churches, but is considered normal in today's society. As the church evolves into a contemporary version of the first century church, we must take a serious look at the collection of money and how it is spent.

## THE SPIRIT OF GIVING

Giving is a reflection of the heart. This truth seems to have been lost in many institutional church settings where 'tithes and offering' have become a weekly ritual. Spiritual gimmicks and manipulative practices are employed to get congregants to turn loose dollars for the church. Giving is induced by guilt, biblical threats or unscriptural promises.

On the other side, I have found that among the organic, simple and house church gatherings giving has all but dried up. This too is a reflection of the heart. I have heard the concerns among this group regarding the continuous lack of financial resources. It seems as though many have retreated into homes and no longer feel obligated to give financially on a regular and consistent basis. It has the appearance of religious selfishness.

> *Remember this: he who sows sparingly will also reap sparingly. He who sows bountifully will also reap bountifully. Let each man give according as he has determined in his heart; not grudgingly, or under compulsion; for God loves a cheerful giver. As it is written, "He has scattered abroad, he has given to the poor. His righteousness remains forever." Now may he who supplies seed to the sower and bread for food, supply and multiply your seed for sowing, and increase the fruits of your righteousness; you being enriched in everything to all liberality, which works through us thanksgiving to God. For this service of giving that you perform not only makes up for lack among the saints, but abounds also through many givings of thanks to God; seeing that through the proof given by this service, they glorify God for the obedience of your confession to the Good News of Christ, and for the liberality of your contribution to them and to all; while they themselves also, with supplication on your behalf, yearn for you by reason of the exceeding grace of God in you. Now thanks be to God for his unspeakable gift! (2Corinthians 9:6-15 World English Bible)*

Paul captured the spirit of giving in his letter to the Corinthian church. The brief discourse above covers five areas that helps us to understand how giving should be done.

1. <u>Believers should sow abundantly</u>. Paul uses agricultural typology to remind believers that their level of giving has direct impact on what they reap (both spiritually and naturally).

2. <u>Believers should give according to the dictates of their heart</u>. Your giving literally exposes your true heart to God. Giving as '*one purposes in his or her heart*' has little to do with the amount given, but rather to the decision to give. He makes it clear that giving under compulsion or grudgingly is fruitless because God responds to cheerful givers.

3. <u>Believer's financial gifts have lasting effects</u>. If a person gives with a pure heart, his or her righteousness – their right standing with God and man – remains forever.

4. <u>Believers are entrusted with 'seed' by God</u>. This is a significant principle. We must never forget that Jesus Christ is Lord over His Church. We are only stewards of what we possess. We must remember that the Holy Spirit orchestrates the activities of the church in the earth – including the flow of resources. As He 'ministers seed to the sower', each sower must discern if what they have received is 'seed' or 'sustenance'. Seed used as the Holy Spirit intends will multiply.

5. <u>Believers understand their giving provides for the needs of fellow believers</u>. Throughout the New Testament, nearly all giving is for the relief of poorer saints (Acts 11:29; Romans 15:26; 2Corinthians 9:9). This leads us to the next important fact.

Giving in the New Testament is rooted in the fifth value of the church – no one lacks among us. Giving is a component of the definition of the church which states that:

**The New Testament Church is an assembly of believers...**

**...<u>who participate in planting and supporting new assemblies of believers to do the same with their prayers, time, finances and</u>**

<u>material resources.</u>

.    It must be the heart felt attitude of every believer that when one saint is lacking among us, all of us lack (1Corinthians 12:25-26). Within each local house church, the believers should insure their brothers and sisters have all they need to be productive in life and ministry. Likewise, each house church should be committed to assisting other members of the local, regional or global Body of Christ. We are a body, fitly joined together, supplying each other with our skills, material resources and finances.

## SHOULD NEW TESTAMENT BELIEVERS TITHE?

If the twenty-first century church is modeling the values, practices and structure of the first century church, is tithing a part of those practices? This is a legitimate question. Some believe tithing is strictly an Old Testament practice, while others view it as an on-going practice in the church. I believe the latter.

If you believe that tithing was a part of the law, then you also know that Jesus did not come to destroy the law but rather to fulfill it. You also know that the righteousness of the law is fulfilled in us (Matthew 5:17; Romans 8:3-4). If you believe that tithing was temporary, then you must explain why it is included in the Levitical discourse, practiced by Israel, commanded in the Malachi-an edicts and never refuted as impractical law by Jesus or the apostles (Genesis 14:19-20; Leviticus 27:30-31; 2Chronicles 31:5; Malachi 3:10). The change from the Old Testament to the New Testament regarding tithes is a change of heart, not a change of practice (Matthew 6:21; 2Corinthians 9:7)

Regular giving was a common practice in the New Testament. Yet, there is little evidence that would label the giving as tithes. Believers in the first century simply gave. Paul even wrote that whoever has a grace to give that they should do so with simplicity (Romans 12:8).

Neither Jesus or the apostles refuted paying tithes. Even when Jesus rebuked the Pharisees for their hypocrisy, He said that tithes should not be left undone, but further implied that there were weightier matters for them to do. He was addressing the hypocrisy of their heart. He did not say it was wrong for them to tithe (Matthew 23:23; Luke 11:42). The writer of Hebrews made it clear that the one who lives forever – Jesus Christ – receives our tithes (Hebrews 7:8). This implies that tithing was still practiced in New Testament times.

Literally, tithing is the tenth part. That was established in the Old Testament. In the New Testament, the principle of giving is not just a tenth, but a recognition that everything we have belongs to the Lord (1Corinthians 10:26). Tithing is a part of our stewardship. As groups gather in homes, tithing should not be neglected. Tithing should not be made a law or mandate, but rather taught and encouraged as a heart felt practice designed to benefit the church.

## BIBLICAL USES OF FINANCIAL RESOURCES

It costs money to operate any church, regardless if it is organic, simple, or institutional. Our goal should be to use funds for things that line up with the examples we find in the Word of God. There is no way that I can outline everything money will be used for, but the following examples may help steer you in the right direction.

The Poor Among Us

*Then the disciples, every man according to his ability, determined to send relief unto the brethren which dwelt in Judaea: (Acts 11:29)*

*For it hath pleased them of Macedonia and Achaia to make a certain contribution for the poor saints which are at Jerusalem. (Romans 15:26)*

*Only they would that we should remember the poor; the same which I also was forward to do. (Galatians 2:10)*

The care of the poor saints should be at the top of our list. The local, regional and national needs of our brothers and sisters must be first. Remember, the church is a living organic entity made up of believers who willingly give to insure that 'no one lacks' among them. That is why Paul instructed believers to *'distribute to the necessity of the saints'* (Romans 12:13; 1Corinthians 16:1; 2Corinthians 9:1,12)

Secondly, giving to the poor in the communities, the region and the world should be another focus of our giving. We should always be ready to meet the needs of the less fortunate.

The church is not a 'welfare' program giving indiscriminately to anyone who has their hand out. Some teach we should give to the poor without restrictions. I disagree. The purpose of our giving should be to position a person to be productive not dependent.

Instructors

*Let him who receives instruction in the Word[of God] share all good things with his teacher [contributing to his support]. (Galatians 6:6Amplified Bible)*

A vibrant New Testament Church will need and have many active five-fold ministry gifts in operation. They will teach in the temple setting, but also to minister from house to house. Paul instructed believers to share financially with those teaching them. The passage above in The Phillips Translation[20] says that *'the man under Christian instruction should be willing to contribute toward the livelihood of his teacher'*. Such giving is voluntary and should never be a prerequisite for ministry service.

Intra-itinerant and itinerant ministers should be willing to serve without any financial remuneration. Their motive must be the building and edifying of the believers. Whatever donation is given to them must be received with thanksgiving and accepted as sufficient.

<u>Money Laid at the Apostles Feet</u>
In the early days of the church following Pentecost, believers gave generously to insure that no one lacked among them. What first appears to be a single incident of laying resources at the Apostles feet is in fact a consistent form of giving with a specific purpose. This type of giving must be understood because a severely dysfunctional version of 'laying money at the apostle's feet' has crept into the modern church.

> *And the multitude of them that believed were of one heart and of one soul: neither said any of them that ought of the things which he possessed was his own; but they had all things common. And with great power gave the apostles witness of the resurrection of the Lord Jesus: and great grace was upon them all. (Acts 4:32-33)*

This type giving begins with the attitude of the believers. They were of one heart and one soul. There was a common belief that individual possessions belonged to the Body of Believers. I want to emphasize that this was not an early form of communism, but rather a *spiritual common-ism* that existed among the believers. Everyone felt that they had all things in common. I believe this includes financial and material resources as well as skills and talents.

Among those I serve, I have witnessed believers sharing vehicles, assisting in repairs, providing labor and much more among each other. I believe this attitude of common-ism is important to the survival of the church. Some may fear that they will be taken advantage of. My response is that when you give your best with a pure heart, God responds to your integrity. If someone is taken advantage of, God will also deal with that matter (1Peter 3:17).

The generous spirit the believers had seemed to have an effect on the preaching of the apostles. The apostles were not encumbered with the individual needs of the believers. They could focus on ministry of the Word. This is why seven men were chosen to handle the distribution of resources (Acts 6:2-4).

*Neither was there any among them that lacked: for as many as were possessors of lands or houses sold them, and brought the prices of the things that were sold, And laid them down at the apostles' feet: and distribution was made unto every man according as he had need. And Joses, who by the apostles was surnamed Barnabas, (which is, being interpreted, The son of consolation,) a Levite, and of the country of Cyprus, Having land, sold it, and brought the money, and laid it at the apostles' feet. (Acts 4:34-37)*

No one lacked among them. Let that thought sink into your spirit. Try to imagine regions of believers wherein no one lacks among them. Imagine a body of believers where every need is met. If it is written in the Word of God, then it is possible to experience.

'*No one lacking...*' was a result of the spirit embraced by the entire community of believers. They believed their possessions were part of the whole community. They had all things in common. Implicit in that belief was the desire that no one should lack among them. Their belief prompted them to act.

Those who had properties and land sold them and brought the proceeds and laid it at the apostle's feet. According to the Jamieson-Fausset-Brown Commentary[21], the act of laying something at someone's feet was most likely a figurative term that implies something that was committed to another's care. In other words, when people laid resources at the apostle's feet, they fully entrusted them with the proper disposition of their giving.

What the apostles did with the money was as important as the act of giving itself. This is where error has crept into the modern version of 'laying money at the apostle's feet'. The money was not used for the benefit of the apostles. The money given was not used to support extravagant lifestyles.

First, the selling of houses and lands, and the subsequent donation of the proceeds was not requested by the apostles. It was the free-will act of believers who obviously saw needs among their brothers and sisters. The apostles understood that they were entrusted with resources that were not intended for them. What they received was given for the needs among the people. Modern day 'apostles' need to take note of this fact. Whenever people put money at an apostle's feet, it is for the needs of believers

Second, the money that was donated was from excess goods sold by the believers. They sold houses and lands. It did not appear to come from the donor's regular source of income. This was a special offering prompted by the Holy Spirit.

I believe this form of giving was on-going and not just a one time event. As believers were led to sell excess items, the proceeds were willingly given to the apostles for distribution. This explains why the lies of Ananias and his wife Sapphira was so grievous (Acts 5:1-11). They lied to the Holy Ghost. They tried to tempt the Spirit of the Lord by holding back a part of what they had sold. The sad irony is that they were not required to give anything. To give or not to give was their choice, and there was no need for them to lie (Acts 5:4). This sin cost them their lives.

Today, in the New Testament Church, donations 'laid at the apostle's feet' should follow the same pattern of the first century church. This type of giving should be prompted by the Holy Spirit and come from the selling or donation of excess goods (i.e. property, houses, cars, clothing, etc). It should always be voluntary. No one should ever be compelled to give in this manner. The funds should be distributed among the saints as needs arise. The local elders should establish guidelines for distributing resources, and local deacons can insure that their policies are carried out equitably.

Elders

*Let the elders that rule well be counted worthy of double honour, especially they who labour in the word and doctrine. For the scripture saith, Thou shalt not muzzle the ox that treadeth out the corn. And, The labourer is worthy of his reward. (1Timothy 5:17-18)*

Should elders be paid, too? Paul implied that providing financial blessing to good elders was in order. The Greek phrase used for double honor (*diplous time*) in 1Timothy 5:17 refers to giving double value. When it is combined with verse 18, it is clear that Paul is speaking about financial remuneration.

Unfortunately some have twisted this passage to suggest the *'senior pastor'* should be paid twice the salary of the highest paid member of the church. This is an erroneous and self-serving interpretation. When you consider the whole counsel of scripture, Paul specifically encouraged elders to be self supporting. He personally set the example.

> *And from Miletus he sent to Ephesus, and called the elders of the church. And when they were come to him, he said unto them, Ye know, from the first day that I came into Asia, after what manner I have been with you at all seasons, Serving the Lord with all humility of mind, and with many tears, and temptations, which befell me by the lying in wait of the Jews: And how I kept back nothing that was profitable unto you, but have shewed you, and have taught you publickly, and from house to house, (Acts 20:17-20)*

> *I have coveted no man's silver, or gold, or apparel. Yea, ye yourselves know, that these hands have ministered unto my necessities, and to them that were with me. I have shewed you all things, how that so labouring ye ought to support the weak, and to remember the words of the Lord Jesus, how he said, It is more blessed to give than to receive. (Acts 20:33-35)*

Peter admonished the elders to serve and shepherd the flock of God willingly, and not for 'filthy lucre'.

> *The elders which are among you I exhort, who am also an elder, and a witness of the sufferings of Christ, and also a partaker of the glory that shall be revealed: Feed the flock of God which is among you, taking the*

*oversight thereof, not by constraint, but willingly; not for filthy lucre,*
*but of a ready mind; (1Peter 5:1-2)*

Jesus warned that some leaders are no more than hirelings. They don't have the interest of the flock in their hearts and they will abandon them when trouble arises.

*But he that is an hireling, and not the shepherd, whose own the sheep are*
*not, seeth the wolf coming, and leaveth the sheep, and fleeth: and the wolf*
*catcheth them, and scattereth the sheep. The hireling fleeth, because he is*
*an hireling, and careth not for the sheep. (John 10:12-13)*

Elders should never serve for money. If they are given financial gifts by the local church, they should receive it with humility. They should not allow gifts to damage their impartiality in overseeing the local church. This is why Paul warned against appointing a novice as an elder. A novice would not know how to handle financial blessings and could easily become caught in the trap of covetousness (1Timothy 3:6). Mature elders who rule well should be counted worthy of double honor by the church they serve.

## Considering Other Paid Staff

In his defense of his apostolic ministry, Paul challenged the Corinthian believers about giving financially to his ministry. In the process of making his case, he made the following statement:

*Do ye not know that they which minister about holy things live of the*
*things of the temple? and they which wait at the altar are partakers with*
*the altar? Even so hath the Lord ordained that they which preach the*
*gospel should live of the gospel. (1Corinthians 9:13-14)*

Paul was referring to the Old Testament priesthood wherein the Levites received the tithes and offerings from all Israel for their care

(Leviticus 6:25-26; Numbers 5:9-10). Unlike the other tribes, the Levites did not receive an inheritance of land. God Himself was their inheritance (Deuteronomy 10:9). Their work began with the Tabernacle in the wilderness and continued in the temple.

The Levites consisted of more than Aaron's son's who served as the primary priests. There were many families among the Levites who served in various capacities (Numbers 3:15-39). They did the work of the temple, and were 'paid' for their work by the other tribes. Let's consider the nature of their work. There were many tasks that were not 'priestly' but necessary for the operation of the Tabernacle.

The New Testament never implies that administration is unnecessary. To the contrary, Paul specifically wrote concerning 'setting in order' things that were amiss. I believe this consisted of both spiritual and operational matters in the churches (1Corinthians 11:34; Titus 1:5).

The fact administrative duties were not highlighted in scripture does not mean they did not exist in the church. How else would you account for Luke knowing how many people were identified as 'being saved' at Pentecost, followed by another specific number of people 'being added' a short time later? This suggests that some records were being kept (Acts 2:41; Acts 4:4). If there were no records or bookkeeping necessary, how could Paul know his needs and the needs of his companions (Acts 20:34)?

Judas was the treasurer for Jesus and the disciples. A treasurer, good or bad must maintain some record of the money (John 12:6; John 13:29). Some scholars believed that Paul dictated his letters and someone else wrote and distributed them. Regarding the book of Colossians, F.F. Bruce made the following observation:

On the point of authorship, Paul and Timothy are named together in the opening salutation as senders of the letter. It has been shown that most of the epistles in which Timothy's name is conjoined in this way with Paul's present some common literary features which mark them off from other letters in the *corpus Paulinum*; a natural explanation of this would be that in these letters Timothy served the apostle as his amanuensis.[22]

For those not familiar with the term *amanuensis* (pronounce ah-man-yoo-entsis), it describes a person who is employed to write from dictation or to copy a manuscript. What F.F. Bruce said is that although Timothy was Paul's son in the Gospel (2Timothy 1:2), and a traveling companion, it seems plausible that Paul possibly paid Timothy to dictate letters to the churches. Again, maybe this is why Paul made it clear that he took care of himself and those who accompanied him (Acts 20:34).

In the Old Testament, we tend to emphasize Moses and Aaron, but God also anointed workmen to build and maintain the Tabernacle (Exodus 35:30-35). Much ado is made about Solomon building the temple, but little consideration is given to Hiram – a skilled behind the scenes worker (1Kings 7:13-14). Ezra, in the Old Testament was a scribe,[23] and the genealogical records in Matthew and Luke are a result of someone keeping records (Matthew 1:1-16; Luke 3:23-38).

We have inadvertently placed so much value on apostles, prophets and other ministry gifts that other behind the scenes workers have become the 'uncomely parts' of the body that are dishonored (1Corinthians 12:20-24). In this season, there are many 'behind the scenes' duties that must be done. The optimum situation is to trust God to raise up those with the passion and skills for things like record keeping, bookkeeping, printing, maintaining websites, etc. God can still fill men and women with ability to fill these needs in the church. When their tasks exceed what can be done on a voluntary basis, then it would be in order to provide compensation for some who would make their living serving the church in this manner.

## Apostles

Offerings should be taken by the local churches to assist itinerant apostles. Like all other offerings, they should be voluntary. There is no biblical evidence that apostles were on the 'payroll' of any local church, but it was clear that churches gave financial support to their work.

Paul addressed this issue with the Corinthian church. He made it clear that if no other church recognized his input into their lives, they surely should (1Corinthians 9:1-2). He then reminds them that he too has the need to eat, drink and maintain a family (vs. 3-4). Yet, it seemed that the Corinthian church left him and Barnabas to fend for themselves (vs. 6). This is a common fear I hear among contemporary apostles. This has led some to create 'apostolic networks' where giving is mandated. I have sadly noted that the 'big donors' in these networks are touted and honored by the 'leading apostle', yet the smaller givers are hardly recognized at all. This modern day practice cannot be found implicitly or explicitly in scripture.

> If we have sown unto you spiritual things, is it a great thing if we shall
> reap your carnal things? If others be partakers of this power over you,
> are not we rather? Nevertheless we have not used this power; but suffer

*all things, lest we should hinder the gospel of Christ. (1Corithians 9:11-12)*

**For a church to neglect financial support of apostles is as wrong as apostles placing demands on the churches for compensation**

Even though Paul poured his life into the Corinthian church, he refused to demand that they support him. His primary motive was the gospel of Christ.

In his letter to the Philippians, Paul wrote the popular scriptures, "*I can do all things through Christ which strengtheneth me*" (Philippians 4:13) and "*... my God shall supply all your need according to his riches in glory by Christ Jesus*" (Philippians 4:19). These statements were in direct relationship to the financial gifts to his work by the Philippian and Macedonian churches.

*I rejoice in the Lord greatly that now at last you have revived your concern for me; indeed, you were concerned for me, but had no opportunity to show it. Not that I am referring to being in need; for I have learned to be content with whatever I have. I know what it is to have little, and I know what it is to have plenty. In any and all circumstances I have learned the secret of being well-fed and of going hungry, of having plenty and of being in need. I can do all things through him who strengthens me. In any case, it was kind of you to share my distress. You Philippians indeed know that in the early days of the gospel, when I left Macedonia, no church shared with me in the matter of giving and receiving, except you alone. For even when I was in Thessalonica, you sent me help for my needs more than once. Not that I seek the gift, but I seek the profit that accumulates to your account. I have been paid in full and have more than enough; I am fully satisfied, now that I have received from Epaphroditus the gifts you sent, a fragrant offering, a sacrifice acceptable and pleasing to God. And my God will fully satisfy every need of yours according to his riches in glory in Christ Jesus. (Philippians 4:10-19 NRSV)*

For a church to neglect financial support of apostles is as wrong as apostles placing demands on the churches for compensation. Modern day apostles should take note of Paul's attitude.

*Receive us; we have wronged no man, we have corrupted no man, we have defrauded no man. (2Corithians 7:2)*

*I robbed other churches by receiving support from them so as to serve you. And when I was with you and needed something, I was not a burden to anyone, for the brothers who came from Macedonia supplied what I needed. I have kept myself from being a burden to you in any way, and will continue to do so. (2 Corinthians 11:8-9 NIV)*

*Behold, the third time I am ready to come to you; and I will not be burdensome to you: for I seek not yours, but you: for the children ought not to lay up for the parents, but the parents for the children. (2Corithians 12:14)*

### The Incorporation Issue
There are many opinions regarding whether or not house, organic or simple churches should incorporate as a non-profit. I personally lean towards incorporating. Let me first give my reasons why we *should not* use corporate laws.

Some people declare their house as a church and parsonage to avoid paying property taxes. Jesus said to render to Caesar (the government) what belongs to them, and render to God what is His (Luke 20:25). Church buildings in most states are exempt from property taxes. This book is advocating a church structure that begins in the houses of believers. I firmly disagree with using the tax laws to avoid paying property taxes on a believer's home simply because they claim it is a church.

Most municipalities use revenues from property taxes to fund needed services to their communities. In the event of a fire, I seriously doubt if a person claiming that his or her home is a church, would deny firefighters access to their home because of their beliefs. If needed, they would call the same police being paid for by the general public's taxes. In my spirit, I see thousands of 'house churches' being planted. For each of them to try and avoid paying property taxes could bring a negative view of the church as a whole, and withhold revenue from the very communities they seek to impact.

In recent years, government funded-faith based grants have been introduced. Many churches have set up 501c3 corporations that are closely tied to their churches. Their 501c3 corporation is technically a separate entity, but often they are run by the founding church.

I am not against faith-based grants. I believe the organizations they fund should be solely stand-alone entities with no direct link to the church. If there are believers who are passionate about a project, and wish to seek government funding, they should do so separate and distinctly from the church.

I have personally served as a Program Director, Director and Executive Director of non-profit corporations. I have run programs that were funded with local, state and federal government grants.

One thing is consistent, whenever the government provides funds, they dictate both usage and policy which can often be in direct conflict with biblical principles.

I knew a Pastor who developed a charter school on his church property. They invested in modular classrooms for the students. When a government representative came to inspect their facility, he instructed the Pastor to place the modular classrooms on his property in such a way that the students would not be able to view the church building. On the other side of the coin, some Pastors brag about finding loopholes in their federal grants that allow them to underwrite pastoral salaries, and the salaries of some of his church workers. This is both unethical and dishonest.

There are two legitimate reasons a local or regional church should incorporate as a non-profit. First, if there is a need to hire paid workers, certain benefits are provided best through the corporate structure (i.e. payroll taxes, workmen's compensation insurance, health insurance, FICA, etc.).

Second, the funds to operate the organization are often the result of individual contributions. Some of these donors may desire an annual record of their giving for tax purposes. Only contributions made to a qualified non-profit entity are eligible for tax write-off. In my opinion, these are the only two reasons for incorporating.

Finally, it is not mandatory that churches incorporate as a 501c3 corporation. In some states, churches can incorporate as a non-profit ecclesiastical corporation – a designation specifically for faith entities. In all cases, I believe these church corporations should be run by volunteer elders who only use the corporate entity as a tool to further the gospel.

# The Kingdom Mandate 13

The earth, a territory of the original creative work, had been decimated by satanic occupation (Genesis 1:1-2). Whatever the earth had been in its original creative state had become a dark and void wasteland that did not fit into the pure creative works of God. It had to be reclaimed.

Out of the deep recesses of endless space a powerful voice reverberated, "Let there be light!" The response was immediate. "...and there was light". The instant response lets us know that right away the power of that voice was understood throughout all eternity (Genesis 1:3-5). At once all eternity knew that God, the King of all that was, is and shall be, had spoken light into existence.

The light was not the incandescent illumination of the sun, moon or stars, as they were not spoken into existence for another three days

(Genesis 1:14-19). Rather, it was a light that would shine within all who understood its source. That light was revelation (Psalms 119:105, 130; 2Peter 1:19). It is light that can only be given by God who speaks it into our 'dark and void' spirits (Matthew 16:17; John 1:1-13; 1Corithians 2:10; 12:3). That light is the revelation of who is in control of all that is past, present and prophesied.

God selected a territory on this damaged, dark and void planet and planted a garden. Not just a simple garden, but a fully supplied territory prepared for His greatest creative work – man, both male and female (Genesis 2:8; Ephesians 2:10). Omniscient, Omnipotent, Omnipresent God created a being fashioned in His Divine Image. As a vessel made from the earth, man was created and designed to hold within him the fullness of God (Colossians 2:9-10). Man was placed in the Garden. The same voice that spoke light into existence now spoke to the man, giving him clear instructions:

> ... and God said unto them, Be fruitful, and multiply, and replenish the earth, and subdue it... (Genesis 1:28)

Man had a mandate. This mandate reflected the purpose of the Kingdom of God – to reclaim the earth from its demonic intruder.

Thousands of years before God the Creator became God the Son declaring "Thy Kingdom come, thy will be done on earth as it is in heaven" – man was given an assignment that would produce Kingdom results in the earth (Matthew 6:10; John 1:1-3, 14; Hebrews 1:1-2). Obedient man could systematically expand the borders of the Garden, until it covered the entire earth. Everything man needed to fulfill his mandate was in the Garden (Genesis 1:29-30).

In a futile attempt to stop his defeat, satan crept into the Garden in the form of a subtle serpent (Genesis 3:1; Ezekiel 28:13). The devil masterfully deceived the woman and the man foolishly rebelled against God his creator. Mankind abdicated their position of authority through a single act of disobedience. The devil seemed to be in control. Defeated and ashamed, man was banished from the Garden (Genesis 3:9-10, 22-24). Yet, God was not deterred from His mission to reclaim the earth. He would redeem man and reposition him to fulfill the original mission to *be fruitful, and multiply, and replenish the earth, and subdue it... (Genesis 1:28).*

## How Would This Be Accomplished?

God's response to man's disobedience would at first seem eternally punitive. Adam and Eve were estranged from God and appeared to be left on their own outside the Garden. The Garden was more than an earthly geographic territory. It was the presence of the Kingdom of God in the earth. It could only be occupied by a select people.

The devil had no rights in the Garden. As long as man obeyed God, the devil had no authority or power in the territory of the Garden. His strategy was to deceive man into relinquishing his rights. When man fell for the bait, satan thought he had gained permanent control. But all he had was the temporal kingdoms – the world systems (Luke 4:5-6; 2Corinthians 4:3-4).

*And the LORD God said unto the serpent, Because thou hast done this, thou art cursed above all cattle, and above every beast of the field; upon thy belly shalt thou go, and dust shalt thou eat all the days of thy life: And I will put enmity between thee and the woman, and between thy seed and her seed; it shall bruise thy head, and thou shalt bruise his heel. (Genesis 3:14-15)*

God decreed that there would be conflict between the '*seed of the woman*', and the '*seed of the serpent*'. It would be a conflict culminating when the head of the serpent is bruised by the heel of the woman's seed.

Through forty-two generations God sent His Son to redeem those who were in bondage (Matthew 1:17; Titus 2:14). His message from the very beginning was repent (change directions), because the Kingdom of Heaven is at hand (Matthew 4:17; 10:7). The devil must have felt this was a futile message. After all, man had been evicted from the Garden, and he had taken control of the world's kingdoms. The kingdoms of business, media, the arts, education, government, the family and even certain religions were under his influence. But all throughout His three and a half years of ministry, Jesus kept preaching the Kingdom (Matthew 4:23; 6:10; 6:33; Luke 9:2; 12:32; John 3:3-5).

The fallen and defeated satan was relentless in his pursuit of Jesus. He tried to destroy Him through religious leaders (John 10:31). He tried to embarrass Him through tarnishing His reputation (John 8:41). He tried to discredit Him with crafty questions (Luke 10:25; 11:53-54). The devil must have thought he succeeded when he found Judas as an ally (Luke 22:3; John 13:2, 27). But he had no clue of what he was doing (1Corinthians 2:8).

After orchestrating a plethora of false witnesses, satan was able to manipulate the religious leaders and Roman government into crucifying Jesus (Mark 14:55-59; Luke 19:1-16). For the followers of Jesus, this looked like total defeat. Jesus, the One who had healed the sick, fed thousands and cast out devils was now beaten beyond recognition, stripped naked and hanging grotesquely on a Roman cross. It looked like the end.

A resolute Joseph of Arimathaea took responsibility for the body of Jesus after His death, just like Joseph, the carpenter took responsibility for Jesus at His birth. Joseph of Arimathaea provided a tomb that had never been used. How ironic that Jesus, born from a virgin's womb was now being buried in a virgin tomb. It was while Jesus' body lay in that tomb that satan began to realize how soundly he had been defeated (1Peter 3:18-19; Revelation 1:18).

Three days after being placed in the tomb, Jesus rose victoriously from the dead (Matthew 28:6; Mark 16:6; Luke 24:6). The head of the serpent – satan – was crushed. The heel of the woman's seed was bruised. It was not a bruising that implied any level of defeat, but rather a bruising for our iniquities, a wounding for our transgression and even the beating He endured was for our healing. In other words, everything satan did against Jesus turned into a source of victory for us (Isaiah 53:5; Colossians 2:15). What satan missed was that his head would be bruised by the heel – which is on the foot of the body (Romans 16:20; 1Corinthians 15:24-25).

The risen Lord could have preached any message after His resurrection. He had all power in both heaven and earth. He had the keys of death and hell. So what was His post-resurrection message? It was the same message He preached at the beginning of His ministry. He preached the same message He preached during His ministry, and clearly His message prior to His ascension. Jesus spent His last forty days on earth preaching the Kingdom of God (Acts 1:3).

The Kingdom of God, first seen as a Garden east of Eden, was again about to be manifested on earth. The Garden was about to be replanted. This time, it would not be located somewhere accessible by flesh. You cannot reference any land map to locate it. This time, God would plant the Kingdom and all its resources in man. On the

Day of Pentecost, the replanting took place when the Holy Ghost swooped in and gave supernatural power to a group of one hundred and twenty believers waiting in an upper room (Luke 12:32; 17:21; Romans 14:17; Ephesians 3:20; Colossians 1:27).

## THE BIRTH OF THE CHURCH

One hundred and twenty were baptized in the Holy Ghost in the upper room. Three thousand were added to them shortly thereafter. Five thousand more joined them within a few weeks. As multiplied thousands began to submit to His Lordship, Jesus Christ spiritually fused these individuals into a living entity – His church – which mystically became known as His Body (Matthew 16:18; Acts 2:47; Ephesians 1:21-22; Colossians 1:18).

The original mandate to be *fruitful, multiply, replenish and subdue* was restored. It is the Kingdom Mandate given to every believer in the church. Every man and woman in Christ, through the power of the Holy Ghost is commissioned to *"...go, and make disciples of all nations, baptizing them in the name of the Father and of the Son and of the Holy Spirit"*.[24] This was not a simple religious suggestion. It is the governmental policy of the Kingdom of God.

This has been the heart of this book, NO LONGER CHURCH AS USUAL. All I have written about structure is futile without understanding the Kingdom Mandate. The structure only houses our activities. The Kingdom Mandate reveals God's purpose. Therefore, everything you have read has been because of the Kingdom Mandate. If you embrace what you have read, then everything you do going forward is because of the Kingdom Mandate.

You are an intricate part of the Universal Body of Christ. You should be a member of a local assembly of believers who form the local church. You are commanded by the Word of God to be fruitful, to multiply, to replenish and to subdue the earth. You are responsible for making disciples. You can do this best by serving in an assembly of believers, who are committed to the Kingdom Mandate.

## THE CHURCH MUST BE FRUITFUL

*Herein is my Father glorified, that ye bear much fruit; so shall ye be my disciples. (John 15:8)*

*Ye have not chosen me, but I have chosen you, and ordained you, that ye should go and bring forth fruit, and [that] your fruit should remain: that whatsoever ye shall ask of the Father in my name, he may give it you. (John 15:16)*

The first active component of the DNA of the church is fruitfulness. This is the first of its reproductive traits. Each component of the church must continually exhibit the ability to replicate itself. Being fruitful is internal multiplication. Specifically, it is causing each member of the Body to be healthy enough to give birth to another like themselves.

## THE CHURCH MUST MULTIPLY

*Then had the churches rest throughout all Judaea and Galilee and Samaria, and were edified; and walking in the fear of the Lord, and in the comfort of the Holy Ghost, were multiplied. (Acts 9:31)*

The principle of numerical growth in the Kingdom is multiplication – not division. A fruitful plant can reproduce another healthy plant. A fruitful disciple produces healthy disciples. A fruitful church plants healthy churches. This is multiplication.

The multiplication of disciples is bringing souls into the Kingdom of God. Making disciples is on-going training and mentoring individuals to be formed into the image of Christ (Romans 8:29; Galatians 4:19). Mature disciples can be sent to plant new assemblies of believers (churches) who repeat the process of making disciples. Two becomes four – four becomes eight – eight becomes sixteen and the multiplication process continues until every community on earth is impacted by the Kingdom of God.

## THE CHURCH MUST REPLENISH OR FILL THE EARTH

The earth is the Lord's and the fullness thereof (Psalms 24:1). The meek shall inherit it (Matthew 5:5). Therefore, the church must pursue the earth. It is our promised inheritance. As with Abraham, we must "Arise, walk in the land through its length and its width, for [God will] give it to [us]" (Genesis 13:17NKJV; Galatians 3:29).

Fruitful, multiplying disciples in fruitful, multiplying churches will naturally fill the earth. As the church grows spiritually, it also grows numerically. Great numbers are added to churches who commit to the Kingdom Mandate.

> Then they that gladly received his word were baptized: and the same day there were added [unto them] about three thousand souls. (Acts 2:41)

> Praising God, and having favour with all the people. And the Lord added to the church daily such as should be saved. (Acts 2:47)

*And believers were the more added to the Lord, multitudes both of men and women. (Acts 5:14)*

## THE CHURCH MUST SUBDUE ANYTHING THAT OPPOSES THE PURPOSES OF GOD

Even in his defeat, satan is still trying to thwart the plan of God. The church must be as militant as it is vigilant in taking territory from the enemy (John 10:10; 1Peter 5:8). We carry the Kingdom and all its resources within us. Our very presence has the potential to release the power of the Kingdom into any situation (Acts 8:5-12; 16:16-20; 17:6). The kingdom is present wherever there are believers demonstrating Kingdom principles over and above the norms of the world.

Just before ascending into heaven, Jesus made sure that believers understood the authority they had in His Name. The power to heal the sick, cast out devils, defy nature, overcome plots and speak with new tongues were the spiritual weaponry given to them to subdue the forces of darkness (Mark 16:17-18; Luke 10:19).

## THE CHURCH: DESTINED FOR DOMINION IN THE EARTH

The Church was in the heart of God from the very beginning. She is the pillar and ground of truth (1Timothy 3:15). Through her, principalities and powers will know the wisdom of God (Ephesians 3:10). As she submits to the Lord Jesus Christ, she is as glorious as she is victorious (Ephesians 5:27).

*But ye shall receive power, after that the Holy Ghost is come upon you: and ye shall be witnesses unto me both in Jerusalem, and in all Judaea, and in Samaria, and unto the uttermost part of the earth. (Acts 1:8)*

The church is a spiritual embassy in the earth filled with Holy Ghost filled ambassadors who each represent some sphere of the Kingdom of God in the earth (1Corinthians 12:4-12; Romans 12:4; 1Thessalonians 2:12). An obedient army of believers will take dominion in the earth (Luke 19:13). You and I are the living fibers bringing life to the Church.

Individually we submit to the Lordship of Jesus Christ. Collectively we mature to the fullness of the stature of Christ. Individually we are to be conformed to the image of Christ. Collectively we are more than conquerors through Jesus Christ. Individually we are members in particular. Collectively we are the Body of Christ. Individually we are lively stones. Collectively we are a holy habitation for the Lord.

This is the Church that Jesus said He would build (Matthew 16:18). This is the Church He gave His life for (Acts 20:28). It is a glorious, powerful magnificent Church. He loves the Church so much that He calls it HIS BRIDE (Revelation 21:9). He identifies with the life and struggles of the Church so much that He calls it HIS BODY (Ephesians 1:22-23). It is *His* Church – the blood washed assembly of believers that this book, NO LONGER CHURCH AS USUAL has been about.

## WHAT WILL YOU DO?

And God said, "Let there be [revelation]. And there was [revelation] (Genesis 1:3). All things were made by him; and without him was not any thing made that was made. In him was life; and the life was the [revelation] of men. And the [revelation] shineth in darkness; and the darkness comprehended it not (John 1:3-5).

The ball is in your court. You must decide if what you have read is human theory or fresh revelation. If it is simply a human idea, you have every right to reject it. But if it is rooted in the Word of God, you must at least determine how what you have read applies to you. The entrance of [God's Word] gives [revelation]; (Psalms 119:130).

Revelation without implementation is futile. If the Lord has spoken to you through this book, I pray He will show you how to walk in the truth you have learned (2Timothy 2:17).

# Where Do You Go From Here? 14

The revelation the Lord has given me is church structure and its importance to the purpose of God. I believe God's purpose in this season is *the work of ministry being done by the saints.*

I understand the danger in releasing any new revelation. Therefore, I am not seeking to start little groups void of oversight. Neither do I desire to start a separatist movement. I simply have a passion to see the purpose of God fulfilled in the earth through the structure of the church demonstrated in the New Testament.

## The Strategy of Isaiah 61

On the morning of December 15, 1991, the Lord gave me the strategy for the work He entrusted to me. It has taken over eighteen years for Him to clearly unfold this strategy to me.

*The Spirit of the Lord GOD is upon me; because the LORD hath anointed me to preach good tidings unto the meek; he hath sent me to bind up the brokenhearted, to proclaim liberty to the captives, and the opening of the prison to them that are bound; To proclaim the acceptable year of the LORD, and the day of vengeance of our God; <u>to comfort all that mourn; To appoint unto them that mourn in Zion</u>, to give unto them beauty for ashes, the oil of joy for mourning, the garment of praise for the spirit of heaviness; <u>that they might be called trees of righteousness, the planting of the LORD</u>, that he might be glorified. <u>And they shall build the old wastes, they shall raise up the former desolations, and they shall repair the waste cities, the desolations of many generations.</u> (Isaiah 61:1-4)*

The entire sixty first chapter of Isaiah consists of declarations and promises pertinent for the church today. In the first four verses, the core of a strategy necessary to fulfill the Kingdom Mandate is revealed.

## ...to comfort all that mourn

It is the Lord's will that none should perish (2Peter 3:9). In His mercy, He sends rain on the just and the unjust (Matthew 5:45). Comforting all that mourn reveals the heart of a loving creator who desires that all of His creation be redeemed.

## ...to appoint unto them that mourn in Zion

This statement reveals the beginning of the divine strategy. God has always chosen to use mankind to accomplish His purposes in the earth. Adam, Noah, Abraham, Moses, David, and Israel as a nation were some who were entrusted by God.

In this passage, Zion received a divine appointment. This is significant. In the time Isaiah wrote this, Zion was known as the City of David. However, it has gone through a distinct progression in its usage in the bible. Today Zion symbolizes the Church.[25] Remember the wisdom of God will be made known by the church (Ephesians 3:10).

The divine will of God is that all who mourn be comforted. Their comfort will come through 'those who mourn in Zion'. This is the strategy. The Spirit of the Lord is sent to comfort all, but only those mourning in Zion receive an assignment to produce it. It is an assignment that results in them being called *'trees of righteousness and the planting of the Lord'*. Then the assignment of the church is revealed.

<u>...they shall build, raise up and repair</u>
The Spirit of the Lord will empower Zion (the church) to rebuild the ancient ruins. They will restore places that have been devastated, and they will renew cities that had been devastated for generations. This is the assignment of the Church, and hopefully this book has shown you the structure the Church needs to embrace to accomplish this work.

> *According to the grace of God which is given unto me, as a wise masterbuilder, I have laid the foundation, and another buildeth thereon. But let every man take heed how he buildeth thereupon (1Corinthians 3:10)*

The only foundation I lay before you is Jesus Christ (1Corinthians 3:11). Yet, like the Apostle Paul I declare 'for this cause' this book has been written to reveal the purpose of Jesus Christ in this season (Ephesians 3:1-4, 14-19).

No Longer Church As Usual is a roadmap. It is my prayer that the Holy Spirit has spoken to you regarding what I have taught you. More importantly, I pray that you will find a place on the foundation from which to build His revelation to you.

## Saturate It With Prayer

My mother, the late Lucille Kurtz would often remind us to "saturate every endeavor with prayer". She taught us that nothing should ever be attempted without seeking the face of the Lord. The work outlined in No Longer Church As Usual demands continuous prayer and fasting to succeed. Writing a book on the subject does not make me an expert. There must still be the daily infusion of instruction from the Holy Spirit.

If you have been stirred to act on what I have taught, I would strongly urge that you first spend some quality time with the Lord. This is not a 'movement' or 'fad'. Pursuing something without the Holy Spirit can reduce even the best of revelations to a 'wind of doctrine'. Please fast and pray first.

After you have a clear release from the Lord, there is still more to pray about. The Holy Spirit must orchestrate the opportunity for this work to proceed. Therefore it is important that you recognize and pray for three significant doors to be opened – a door of ministry, a door of utterance and a door of faith[26].

A Door of Ministry

*For a great door and effectual is opened unto me, and there are many adversaries (1Corinthians 16:9)*

*Furthermore, when I came to Troas to preach Christ's gospel, and a door was opened unto me of the Lord (2Corinthians 2:12)*

To assume that you can introduce fresh revelation anywhere and anytime can be a serious mistake. The opportunity to begin a work comes only after the Holy Spirit has opened a door of ministry – a platform from which to present the Lord's will.

It would also be a mistake to believe that new truth will be readily accepted. Paul said a 'great door and effectual' had been opened unto him, and there were many adversaries. In other words, every opportunity will be accompanied by objectors. Everyone will not embrace 'the present truth'. That is a fact of ministry. Therefore, we should pray for the Lord to open a door of ministry for His work to be presented, and then minister in the place He has provided.

## A Door of Utterance

*Withal praying also for us, that God would open unto us a door of utterance, to speak the mystery of Christ, for which I am also in bonds (Colossians 4:3)*

As the Lord opens a door of ministry for His work, we should fervently pray for a door of utterance. Paul described this as the ability to speak the mysteries of Christ. Fresh revelation requires those who can articulate it with clarity.

When the Lord first began to share the revelation of church structure and its relationship to the work of ministry, I attempted to share the revelation with several people. Often I received bewildered reactions from those I spoke to, including those in my local church gathering. I even invited a guest speaker who was a strong advocate of the simple church. I thought he could reinforce what I had been sharing. As much as he tried, his message fell on deaf ears. In fact, some were offended by his teaching. The Lord had not opened a door of utterance to me or him at that time.

When I understood the importance of the door of utterance, I taught it to the intercessors who have been praying for it on a consistent basis. The result has been impressive. By God's grace I have received new levels of revelation regarding His purposes. I cannot open the bible and not see church structure and how it relates to the work of ministry being done by the saints. Moreover, what I see in my spirit, the Holy Spirit has given me clear ways to articulate it. There are many in our local gathering who have expressed their excitement regarding this revelation. I attribute the writing of this book to God providing a door of utterance to me.

Paul said that with the door of ministry came many adversaries. I have found that when the door of ministry is combined with the door of utterance, the Holy Spirit will expose the adversaries and give strategies to overcome them. Adversaries are never to be the defeat of any work of God. This leads to the third strategic door.

<u>The Door of Faith</u>

*And when they were come, and had gathered the church together, they rehearsed all that God had done with them, and how he had opened the door of faith unto the Gentiles (Acts 14:27)*

The door of ministry is when the Holy Spirit provides the place where God's work will take place. The door of utterance is the Holy Spirit giving the ability to articulate the work. Finally, the Holy Spirit must open a door of faith in the territory of the ministry, so that the door of utterance can effectively be received. This should be another focus of daily prayer.

The door of faith opens when the Holy Spirit moves upon a person or group of people to receive the Word of the Lord. Fresh revelation is readily accepted when the Holy Spirit releases the faith to receive it (Romans 12:3; Ephesians 2:8).

Paul's prayer for the church in Ephesus was that 'the eyes of [their] understanding [would be] enlightened; that [they would] know what is the hope of his calling, and what the riches of the glory of his inheritance in the saints, And what is the exceeding greatness of his power to [them] who believe, according to the working of his mighty power' (Ephesians 1:18-19). In essence, he prayed that the Lord would open a door of faith to them.

Before any work of the Lord is attempted, we must be willing to pray for Him to open the doors of ministry, utterance and faith so that our efforts will be effective. This is first step in accomplishing God's will in the earth.

## STRATEGIC BUILDING OF TERRITORIES

We cannot limit the methods God will use to reach any area. Our only responsibility is to be obedient to Him. Scripture gives many examples of how the Holy Spirit orchestrated reaching the lost, and expansion of the Kingdom of God in the earth.

The revelation I have is to do the work you have read about in this book on a regional basis.

> For we are not bold to class or compare ourselves with some of those who commend themselves; but when they measure themselves by themselves, and compare themselves with themselves, they are without understanding. But we will not boast beyond our measure, but within

*the measure of the sphere which God apportioned to us as a measure, to*
*reach even as far as you. For we are not overextending ourselves, as if we*
*did not reach to you, for we were the first to come even as far as you in*
*the gospel of Christ; not boasting beyond our measure, that is, in other*
*men's labors, but with the hope that as your faith grows, we shall be,*
*within our sphere, enlarged even more by you, so as to preach the gospel*
*even to the regions beyond you, and not to boast in what has been*
*accomplished in the sphere of another. (2 Corinthians 10:12-16 New*
*American Standard Version)*

When the Lord instructed me to write this book, He made it clear that I should not publish the inaugural edition for national distribution. Too many books have been written from theory rather than experience. This book must first end up in the hands of those who are most apt to do this work in the immediate geographic region He has given to me. The success of this work is contingent upon me staying within the measure God has given to me. If it is to go worldwide, it will only happen as we obey God in the territories where He has opened a door of ministry, a door of faith and has given us a door of utterance.

## WORTHY ONE AND THE SON OF PEACE

*And into whatsoever city or town ye shall enter, enquire who in it is*
*worthy; and there abide till ye go thence. And when ye come into an*
*house, salute it. And if the house be worthy, let your peace come upon it:*
*but if it be not worthy, let your peace return to you (Matthew 10:11-13)*

*And into whatsoever house ye enter, first say, Peace be to this house.*
*And if the son of peace be there, your peace shall rest upon it: if not, it*

*shall turn to you again. And in the same house remain, eating and drinking such things as they give: for the labourer is worthy of his hire. Go not from house to house. (Luke 10:5-7)*

One concept Jesus set forth was to seek out and find the 'worthy ones' and 'son of peace' in a community. These are individuals who embrace the apostolic workers and their message. It is possible that these individuals can be influential and have the capacity to open avenues of outreach in a region. I personally will be praying for existing pastors to embrace this transition. In my opinion, the best scenario would be work with an existing church desiring to convert to the New Testament structure.

*And a vision appeared to Paul in the night; There stood a man of Macedonia, and prayed him, saying, Come over into Macedonia, and help us. And after he had seen the vision, immediately we endeavoured to go into Macedonia, assuredly gathering that the Lord had called us for to preach the gospel unto them (Acts 16:9-10).*

Paul's vision regarding helping the saints in Macedonia shows us another way to reach into new territories. The Holy Spirit may show us areas He wants to effect through dreams and visions. It then becomes our responsibility to trust God to open the doors of ministry, utterance and faith.

I also believe the Lord has given me to believe Him for 120 believers in each territory. Although I understand how this number can be applied to those in the upper room (Acts 1:15), or the promised life of man (Genesis 6:3) or the purported number of years Noah preached, this is no magical number. It is simply the number of believers I believe the Lord has given me to reach in each territory.

## TRAINING

Finally, the most important task before me or any apostle in any ministry work is to train workers who will maintain it when it has become mature. Training will take time, but is crucial to the success of the work.

### Elders

Without question, elders must be trained first. They will have the responsibility to govern the local church. These men must be appointed and developed according to biblical standards. Please review chapter eight to understand the magnitude of all that is expected of an elder.

### Home Leaders

The house church gatherings are the foundation of the church in a city and region. Churches will need to be planted in homes where there is a clear understanding of New Testament structure and values. Each house church must be taught how to build relationships and look forward to planting other gatherings.

### Ascension Gifts

The development of the saints is done by the ascension gifts. Those identified within a territory can be trained by existing ascension gifts from other territories. This will insure that there is continuity in what is taught in all the local churches.

## THE BALL IS IN YOUR COURT

*[You have been] raised up in righteousness, and I will direct all [your] ways: [you] shall build my city, and [you] shall let go my captives, not for price nor reward, saith the LORD of hosts (Isaiah 45:13)*

On March 23, 1994 the above passage was prophesied to me. While in prayer on August 22, 1995 He reminded me of this word and instructed me to embrace it as my personal apostolic mandate for ministry.

I must live in right standing with God and man. I must totally be led by the Holy Spirit in everything I do. I must be a builder of God's City – Zion – the Church. I must provide a viable outlet for all the ministry gifts. Finally, everything I do must be done without motivation for financial gain or human accolades. I attempt everyday to obey this mandate. My heart is for the church of my Lord Jesus Christ.

I have no desire to build my own kingdom. I close this book by putting the ball into your court. Are you ready to experience the 'unusual church'? Are you ready to see the work of ministry being done by millions of saints in the earth? Are you ready for the Kingdom Mandate to be fulfilled?

The church is in transition. It is not a house, simple or organic church movement. It is a return to first century structure and values. It is the Holy Spirit highlighting the work of ministry to be done by the saints.

The restoration of salvation by grace through faith has been restored to the church. Holiness, sanctification, water baptism and the gifts of the Spirit have been restored to the church. The ascension gifts of the apostle, prophet, evangelist, pastor and teacher have been restored to the church to mature the saints for the work of ministry.

The stage is now set to establish the Church Jesus gave His life for. Are you the missing link the Holy Spirit is looking for to launch NO LONGER CHURCH AS USUAL right now?

# Index

# ENDNOTES

[1] Dr. Bill Hamon THE DAY OF THE SAINTS: *Equipping Believers for their Revolutionary Role in Ministry* © 2002 Page 248 Destiny Image Publishers

[2] The Robertson's Word Pictures of the New Testament © Broadman Press 1932,33, Renewal 1960. All rights reserved.

[3] Dr. Kevin J. Connor, *The Church In The New Testament* © 1989 KJC Publications/Bible Temple Publishing Pages 195-210

[4] Watchman Nee THE NORMAL CHRISTIAN CHURCH LIFE: *The New Testament Pattern of the Churches, the Ministry and the Work* © 1980 Living Steams Ministry, Page 52

[5] See comforter and exhort *Vines Expository Dictionary of New Testament Words*

[6] Gene A. Getz ELDERS AND LEADERS: *God's plan for leading the church* © 2003 Moody Publishers Page 42

[7] Ibid Page 96

[8] Kevin J. Connor THE CHURCH IN THE NEW TESTAMENT © 1989 Sovereign World, LTD Bible Temple Publishing Pages 111-117

[9] This by no means is the first mention of elders in the scriptures, but it is the first mention of elders in connection with the church. This took place around A.D. 45. It must also be noted that correspondence was sent to the elders – not just the saints.

[10] Kevin Connor *THE CHURCH IN THE NEW TESTAMENT* © 1989 Bible Temple Publishing Page 122

[11] Dr. Greg Ogden UNFINISHED BUSINESS: *Returning The Ministry To The People Of God* © 1990,2003 Published by Zondervan, Refer to Chapter 6 pages 130 - 155

[12] Watchmen Nee THE NORMAL CHRISTIAN CHURCH LIFE: *The New Testament Pattern of the Churches, the Ministry, and the Work* © 1980 Living Stream Ministry Page 6

[13] Kevin J. Connor THE CHURCH IN THE NEW TESTAMENT © 1989 Bible Temple Publishing Page 170

[14] The word *servant* in this text is translated from the word Greek word doulos which means 'slave or bond servant'

[15] The Greek word translated into bishop is *episkopos* which describes the work of an elder.

[16] But I say unto you, That ye resist not evil: but whosoever shall smite thee on thy right cheek, turn to him the other also. (Matthew 5:39 KJV)

[17] Tim Kurtz, PROPHETIC JUDGMENT: *Discerning Personal Prophecy* © Kingdom Word Publications 2002

[18] Luther's 36th Thesis: Every truly repentant Christian has a right to full remission of penalty and guilt, even without letters of pardon.

[19] Luther's 86th Thesis: "Why does not the pope, whose wealth is to-day greater than the riches of the richest, build just this one church of St. Peter with his own money, rather than with the money of poor believers?"

[20] Geoffrey Bles, LTD. *The New Testament in Modern English* Copyright © 1960 by J.B. Phillips

[21] See notes Acts 4:35 Jamieson-Fausset-Brown Commentary on the Whole Bible

[22] F.F. Bruce, *Paul: Apostle Of The Heart Set Free* © 1977 The Paternoster Press, Ltd. Page 408

[23] Scribes were members of a learned class in ancient Israel through New Testament times who studied the Scriptures and served as copyist, editors and teachers. (*See Nelson's Illustrated Bible Dictionary*)

[24] Matthew 28:18 from the World English Bible Version

[25] See Illustrated Bible Dictionary Copyright © 1986 Thomas Nelson Publishers

[26] The three-fold principle of 'the door of utterance, the door of ministry and the door of faith' was originally taught by Brother Gbile Akanni and included in his book, WHAT GOD LOOKS FOR IN A VESSEL. Published 1999 by Peace House Publications, Gboko, Benue State, Nigeria

# Bibliography

Unless otherwise indicated, the **Authorized King James Version** is used for scripture references. The following bibles were used for additional clarity and continuity of doctrinal thought.

THE AMPLIFIED BIBLE, EXPANDED EDITION
Copyright © 1987 by The Zondervan Corporation

THE BIBLE: JAMES MOFFATT TRANSLATION *by James A.R. Moffatt*
Copyright © 1922, 1924, 1925, 1926, 1935 by Harper Collins San Francisco
Copyright © 1950, 1952, 1953, 1954 by James A.R. Moffatt

THE COMPARATIVE STUDY BIBLE
Copyright © 1984 by The Zondervan Corporation

THE HEBREW GREEK KEY STUDY BIBLE
*King James Version*
Copyright © 1984, 1991 by AMG International, Inc.

THE WORD: THE BIBLE FROM 26 TRANSLATIONS
Copyright © 1988, 1991, 1993 Mathis Publishers, Inc.


## CONCORDANCES, LEXICONS AND REFERENCE BOOKS

ACTS: AN INDEPENDENT STUDY by Irving L. Jensen, Copyright © 1968 The Moody Bible Institute of Chicago

BARNES NOTES ON THE NEW TESTAMENT by Albert Barnes, Copyright © 1962, 1963, 1966, 1968

BIBLE DOCTRINES: REVISED EDITION by P.C. Nelson, Copyright © 1948, 1971, revised 1981 Gospel Publishing House

DICTIONARY OF BIBLICAL IMAGERY by [various editors], Copyright © 1998 by Intervarsity Christian Fellowship

HALLEY'S BIBLE HANDBOOK by Henry H. Halley, Twenty-Fourth Edition, Copyright © 1965 by Halley's Bible Handbook, Inc.

INTERPRETING THE SYMBOLS AND TYPES: COMPLETELY REVISED AND EXPANDED
Copyright © 1980 by Kevin J. Connor

Dr. Martin Luther's Small Catechism: A Handbook of Christian Doctrine Copyright © 1943 Concordia Publishing House

Nelson's Illustrated Bible Dictionary by Herbert Lockyer, Sr. and [various editors]. Copyright © 1986 Thomas Nelson Publishers

The Church in the New Testament by Kevin J. Connor KJC Publications

The New Strong's Exhaustive Concordance of the Bible by James Strong, LL.D., S.T.D. Copyright © 1995, 1996 by Thomas Nelson Publishers

Vine's Expository Dictionary of New Testament Words: Unabridged Edition by W.E. Vine, M.A. MacDonald Publishing Company

Vine's Expository Dictionary of Old and New Testament Words by W.E. Vine, Old Testament Edited by F.F. Bruce Copyright © 1981 by Fleming H. Revell a Division of Baker Book House Company

Zondervan Compact Bible Dictionary Copyright © 1993 by Zondervan Publishing House

## SUGGESTED READING

Allen, Roland *Missionary Methods St. Paul's or Ours?* © 1962 World Dominion Press

Atkerson, Steve [Editor], *House Church: simple – strategic – scriptural* © 2008 New Testament Reformation Fellowship

Barna, George *Revolution: Finding Vibrant Faith Beyond the Wall of the Sanctuary*, Tyndale House Publishers, Inc.

Beckham, William A. *The Second Reformation: Reshaping the Church for the 21st Century*, Touch Publications

Bismark, Tudor *Order in the House: Establishing God's Governmental Structure in the Church and Beyond*, Truebrand Marketing Group

Bismark, Tudor *Reformation in the House: An Apostolic Model for the 21st Century Church*, Truebrand Marketing Group

Bright, John *The Kingdom of God*, Abingdon Press

Bruce, F.F. *Paul: Apostle of the Heart Set Free*, William B. Eerdmans Publishing Company

Castellanos, Cesar *Successful Leadership through the Government of 12: Revised Edition*, G12 Publishers

Choudrie, Victor *Greet the Ekklesia: The Church in Your House*, English Addition July 2006

Clements, Dr. Kirby *A Philosophy of Ministry*, Publisher unknown

Clements, Dr. Kirby *When Prophecies Fail: A Practical Response to the Voice of God*, Clement Family Ministries

Cole, Neil *Organic Church: growing faith where life happens*, Jossey Bass

Cooke, Graham/Goodell, Gary *Permission Granted: to do Church differently in the 21ˢᵗ Century*, Destiny Image ® Publishers

Dale, Felicity *Getting Started, second edition* Karis Publishing

David, Jonathan *Apostolic Strategies Affecting Nations*, 1997 Edition

Eckhardt, John *Moving in the Apostolic*, Renew Books Gospel Light

Eckhardt, John *Presbyteries and Apostolic Teams*, Crusaders Ministries

Eckhardt, John *The Ministry Anointing of the Apostle*, Crusaders Ministries

Getz, Gene A. *Elders and Leaders: God's Plan for Leading the Church: A Biblical, Historical and Cultural Perspective*, Moody Publishers

Hamon, Dr. Bill *Apostles Prophets and the Coming Moves of God: God's End-Time Plans for His Church and Planet Earth*, Destiny Image ® Publishers

Hamon, Dr. Bill *The Day of the Saints: Equipping Believers for their Revolutionary Role in Ministry*, Destiny Image ® Publishers

Hamon, Dr. Bill *The Eternal Church: A Prophetic Look at the Church – Her History, Restoration, and Destiny*, Destiny Image ® Publisher

Hamon, Dr. Bill, *Prophets Pitfalls and Principles: God's Prophetic People Today*, Destiny Image ® Publishers

Hamon, Jane *The Cyrus Decree: Releasing apostolic and prophetic keys to the twenty-first century Church to liberate captives, transfer wealth, revolutionize nations and build the Kingdom of God*, Christian International Family Church

Joyner, Rick *A Prophetic Vision for the 21ˢᵗ Century: A Spiritual Map to Help You Navigate into the Future*, Thomas Nelson Publishers

Kraybill, Donald B. *The Upside Down Kingdom*, Herald Press

Krieder, Larry/Myer, Ron/Prokopchak, Steve/Sauder, Brian *The Biblical Role of Elders for Today's Church: New Testament leadership principles for equipping elders*, House to House Publications

Kurtz, Apostle Tim *How to discover your Calling, Purpose & Ministry*, Kingdom Word Publications

Kurtz, Apostle Tim *Prophetic Judgment: Discerning Personal Prophecy*, Kingdom Word Publications

Munroe, Myles *God's Big Idea: Reclaiming God's Original Purpose for Your Life*, Destiny Image ® Publishers

Nee, Watchman *The NORMAL CHRISTIAN CHURCH LIFE: The New Testament Pattern of the Churches, the Ministry, and the Work*, Living Stream Ministry

Ogden, Greg *Unfinished Business: Returning the Ministry to the People of God*, Zondervan

Rutz, James *Mega Shift*, Empowerment Press

Rutz, James *Open Church*, Empowerment Press

Sapp, Roger *The Last Apostles on Earth*, All Nations Publications

Simson, Wolfgang *Houses That Change the World: The return of the house churches*, Authentic Books

Slaughter, Michael *Spiritual Entrepreneurs: 6 Principles for Risking Renewal*, Abingdon Press

Slaughter, Michael/Bird, Warren *unLearing Church: just when you thought you had leadership all figured out*, Group Publishing

Trueblood, Elton *The Company of the Committed: A bold and imaginative rethinking of the strategy of the Church in contemporary life*, Harper & Row Publishers

Viola, Frank *So You Want To Start A House Church? First Century Style Church Planting For Today*, Present Testimony Ministry

Viola, Frank/Barna, George *PAGAN Christianity? Exploring the roots of our church practices – Revised and Updated*, Tyndale House Publishers

Weston, Charles Gilbert *The Seven Covenants: A Study of The Bible Through The Seven Great Covenants of The Scriptures*, Weston Bible Ministries

Wohlberg, Steve *End Time Delusions: The Rapture, the Antichrist, Israel, and the End of the World*, Treasure House/Destiny Image ® Publishers

# OTHER BOOKS BY TIM KURTZ

APOSTOLIC AWAKENING

PROPHETIC JUDGMENT *How Judge Personal Prophecy*

How to discover your CALLING, PURPOSE AND MINISTRY

## To Order:

www.ntcdonline.org/resources

Want to know more about becoming a church that reflects the values and structure of the first century church? Here's what you can do:

1. <u>Pray</u>. Seek the Lord first. Commit to being led by the Holy Spirit in this matter.

2. <u>Seek the Word of God</u>. This book was written to give you an overview of what scripture says about the values and structure of the church. This book does not take the place of your personal study of the Word of God regarding the Lord's Church.

3. <u>Contact THE CENTER FOR NEW TESTAMENT CHURCH DEVELOPMENT</u>. We would be honored to pray with you, answer your questions and discuss this with you personally. Email us at <u>info@ntcdonline.org</u> or visit our website at <u>www.ntcdonline.org</u>

LaVergne, TN USA
17 September 2010
197447LV00002B/22/P